The Vaudois of

A Visit to Their Valleys

J. N. Worsfold

Alpha Editions

This edition published in 2024

ISBN : 9789362925121

Design and Setting By
Alpha Editions
www.alphaedis.com
Email - info@alphaedis.com

As per information held with us this book is in Public Domain.
This book is a reproduction of an important historical work. Alpha Editions uses the best technology to reproduce historical work in the same manner it was first published to preserve its original nature. Any marks or number seen are left intentionally to preserve its true form.

Contents

PREFACE. .... - 1 -
CHAPTER I. .... - 2 -
CHAPTER II. .... - 5 -
CHAPTER III. .... - 7 -
CHAPTER IV. .... - 10 -
CHAPTER V. .... - 15 -
CHAPTER VI. .... - 18 -
CHAPTER VII. .... - 24 -
CHAPTER VIII. .... - 28 -
CHAPTER IX. .... - 32 -
CHAPTER X. .... - 38 -
CHAPTER XI. .... - 54 -
CHAPTER XII. .... - 58 -
CHAPTER XIII. .... - 63 -
CHAPTER XIV. .... - 69 -
CHAPTER XV. .... - 72 -

PREFACE.

An eminent living scholar, Dr. Tischendorf, has remarked, that in these days there is need of "little books on great subjects." It was something of that feeling which led me to the idea of supplementing the large and learned works of Muston, Monastier, Gilly, and others, by a pocket volume, so small that the tourist might not feel it an incumbrance, and yet so comprehensive, that those who have not the leisure for larger works, might obtain useful knowledge of the Waldenses.

Whether I shall have succeeded in this aim the public must judge.

I may, however, add that the absorbing nature of my parochial work has prevented my doing justice to the subject, from a literary point of view, and, therefore, I must ask my readers to kindly think of it merely as an earnest desire to diminish somewhat of the lack of information which I have discovered even among educated and benevolent persons, with regard to the history and ecclesiastical character of the Vaudois.

And, secondly, to evoke help towards their work generally, but especially to call out contributions, by means of which a MEMORIAL CHURCH may be erected near the site of the ancient college of the Vaudois, at Pra del Tor, Val Angrogna, and so still further illustrate the accuracy of the ancient motto of the Vaudois, "The hammers are broken, the anvil remains."

"TRITUNTUR MALLEI REMANET INCUS."

13, Oakley Square, N.W., July, 1873.

CHAPTER I.

Early on the morning of Easter Monday, 1871, in company with a devoted Italian pastor, I left my temporary home in the comfortable "Grand Hotel," in the little town of Pallanza, to gratify a long-felt desire of visiting that part of Europe made sacred by ages of heroic suffering and courageous endurance for faith and fatherland—the valleys of Piedmont. As we steamed up the lake Maggiore the thin mist of early morn cleared off, and by the time we had passed the far-famed Borromean Islands the eye was ravished with the scenes of beauty on every side. Trees and flowers bloomed forth in the lovely vesture of an Italian spring, and the hills, villas, and gardens on the shores of the lake were imaged forth as in a mirror on its own fair bosom.

In this reverie of delight our boat landed us at Arona, where we disembarked and entered the train for Turin. We reached the latter city in about three hours, and after a short delay at the refreshment-room, called upon the Vaudois pastor, the Rev. J. P. Meille, who received us most kindly, and showed us over the stately temple belonging to his church, situated in one of the best streets (the Corso del Re), and which, by its imposing character, as compared with the general simplicity of the Vaudois ecclesiastical buildings, fitly illustrates their altered circumstances as a Church and a community—no longer persecuted, plundered, proscribed, and downtrodden!

The erection of this building was indeed the first public and palpable evidence that the era of political and religious liberty for the Waldenses, inaugurated by the edict of emancipation, dated February 17th, 1848, was really to be enjoyed by them. Its foundations were laid on the 29th October, 1851, by a solemn ceremonial. Delegates from the table of the Vaudois Church, the consistory of Turin, and all the representatives of Protestant states, together with a numerous concourse of sympathizers and lookers-on, were present. This great innovation upon the long reign of intolerance was not accomplished without considerable effort. In the first place, it was necessary to obtain the authorization of the government, and this was the more difficult from the circumstance that liberty of conscience and public worship were not *formally* inscribed on the "*Statuto*," so that the government might have refused the authorization, and yet not have violated the strict letter of the law. Happily, however, the president of the council of ministers at that time was the Count Cavour, whose influence procured the necessary permission. Many attempts, however, were made to undo this concession, and even when the royal sanction had been obtained these efforts were so numerous and influential that nothing but the proverbial justice of the sovereign, and the constancy of his minister, availed to secure success. The last piece of opposition to the desire of the Vaudois and their friends was made by a man whose name remained as the living incarnation of the former régime, the Count Solaro Margherita, who, during the long years under the reign of Charles Albert, had held the helm of the state, and was completely in bondage to the Jesuits. Though infirm in body, he betook himself to the presence of the successor of his ancient master, and falling on his knees, said to him, "Sire, do not refuse one of the most faithful servants of your dynasty the last favour that he will ask of you before he quits this earth, viz., that you do not allow the good and loyal city of Turin to have the grief and shame of seeing erected within its walls an edifice set apart for the preaching of heresy." (See MEILLE'S *Life of Gen. Beckwith*.) The king referred the suppliant to his ministers, who never dreamt of recalling their decision, and the good work proceeded. So that within a little over two years from its commencement the dedication of the temple took place, on the 15th of December, 1853. There was a great gathering of all ranks of society, including the greater portion of the diplomatique body resident in Turin, the senators, the deputies, a delegation from the national guard of the city with their officers at their head. This last circumstance seems to have given special umbrage to the more bigoted Romanists, inasmuch as their organ, *L'Armonia*, wrote as follows:—"The 15th of December will be written among the most disgraceful in the annals of Piedmont—*the Eighth Anniversary of the Immaculate Conception*, and the Valdesi have appointed it as the day for the solemn opening of the Protestant temple." And it goes on to say, those who have ordered the national guard to take part in the ceremony "have attempted to dishonour the city militia."

But gratifying as it was to me to contemplate this sacred edifice, yet we were anxious not to lose time in reaching the valleys, so we left by the afternoon train for Pinerolo, a town of ominous memories as regards its past connection with its Protestant neighbours. Missionaries, monks, and soldiers have often started forth from this point to molest or destroy those whose virtues they should rather have endeavoured to imitate. The last enterprise of this kind was brought about by the instigation of Archbishop Charvaz of Pinerolo, during the years 1840-1844.

From the railway station at Pinerolo we changed our conveyance, and took a seat on the outside of the diligence for La Torre. On our way we passed the small towns of San Secondo, celebrated as the place where a Christian martyr suffered in the third century, Bricherasio, where deeds of violence were perpetrated against those whose forefathers owned the soil from which their children have been long excluded. Although the shades of evening were closing over us ere we finished our journey, yet we could not fail to be impressed with the nature of the territory to which we were drawing nigh. Monte Viso reared its snow-crested cone with a seeming sense of its majesty. It has been beautifully described as looking like a pyramid starting out of a sea of mountain ridges, and from certain points of view to surpass even Mont Blanc in grandeur, inasmuch as it stands out in larger space, and so makes a more powerful impression on the senses. Although but 12,000 feet high, no one has been able to scale the summit of its gigantic rocks. "Free from the tread of human foot, it is the Jungfrau of the South, the powerful spirit which watches over our valleys; for in the shade of its granite sides the torch of the gospel found refuge for its light." Full of grand emotions as we neared the spot, our diligence brought us to the little capital, La Torre Pelice, where, under the hospitable roof of the Bear Hotel, we rest for the night.

CHAPTER II.

Before narrating my personal adventures in the valleys, I fancy I may consult the profit of my readers if I give a brief topographical outline of the district of which La Torre is the chief town. It lies about thirty miles south-west of Turin, having Mont Viso and the French province of Dauphiny for its south-western border. Mont Genevre is the extreme point in the north-westerly direction, and from its sides the boundary of the upper portions of the valleys turns in a north-easterly direction along that ridge of the Alps which separates Savoy from Piedmont by the Col de Sestrieres, Fenestrelle, Perousa, down to the plains, including the valleys of Pragela, San Martino, Perousa, Angrogna, and Pelice, or Lucerna, and terminating with the parish of San Giovanni as its most easterly point; though formerly the Vaudois territories extended to the entire valley of the Clusone, and they had several churches in the neighbourhood of Susa, as well as in the principality of Saluzzo to the south-east. However, persecution and confiscation have now reduced them to a tract which is about twenty-two miles in its greatest length by a little over sixteen in its extreme width. Its area may be about three hundred square miles, and as so large a space is covered with mountains, it imposes considerable difficulties in the way of productive cultivation. Its population is about twenty thousand persons, which at one time were almost exclusively Protestant, but the disabilities imposed on the Vaudois (of which we shall speak in another chapter) have compelled many of them to leave their native valleys for France, Germany, America, and other countries, in order to obtain a livelihood. As regards scenery, it is difficult to describe its surpassing loveliness, and certainly no exaggeration to say that the traveller in this district is often favoured by a combination most delightful, viz., the soft luxuriance of Italy in the lower slopes and broader valleys, joined with the wildness and grandeur of Switzerland in the narrower glens and loftier mountain ranges. And this apart from the wealth of its historic glories. In reference to climate, the valleys of Pelice, Angrogna, with Perousa, are warm and productive, those of Martino and Pragela cold and barren. The soil in the mountain parishes yields the same kind of vegetables and corn as are to be found in our North of England parishes; the mountain slopes yield pasturage for cattle, and the higher ridges are covered with the pine, elm, and ash trees. In the lower valleys, particularly in the parishes of San Giovanni, Lucerna, La Torre, you will observe the chestnut, mulberry, and the vine. As to roads and means of communication, there is nothing to complain of, particularly from the month of June to September; though I found it so hot in the month of April as to be obliged to stay in-doors from noon to about four o'clock in the afternoon. As to accommodation for travellers, I can speak well of the Bear Hotel at La Torre; and I have read a good account of the Sun at Perousa, as likewise the Red Rose at Fenestrelle, for passing travellers. Having given the above with a view of answering questions often asked, especially by intending tourists, I return to the story of my own observations in La Torre. The place is not unlike other small towns in the Swiss cantons. There are a fair sprinkling of shops, with post-office, town-hall, and market-place. In the centre of the latter I observed a prominent sun-dial, with the following very appropriate motto, *Vita fugit sicut umbra*.

CHAPTER III.

THE ORIGIN AND ANTIQUITY OF THE WALDENSES.

After enquiring as to the geographical position of the Waldensian valleys, the next most frequent questions which arise are: Who are the Waldenses? how long have they been in the valleys of Piedmont? what circumstances led to their taking up their abode there? and what has given to their history that peculiar characteristic which makes every detail both of their past and present so intensely interesting to all the lovers of piety and patriotism wherever the story of their high-souled courage or their long-enduring faith has reached? It is to answer these questions, as briefly and yet as accurately as possible, that we address ourselves in this chapter.

And, first of all, we would state very distinctly that there is no ground for believing that their name of Waldenses is taken from that of Peter Waldo, the celebrated merchant of Lyons. Not only because they date their origin centuries before his time, but also because the names they bear of Waldenses, Vaudois, and Valdesi all refer to the place of their abode, and not to that of any individual whose opinions they had embraced, or whose leadership they had followed. It may further be observed, in opposition to the opinion of the Waldenses being named after Peter Waldo, that his second name does not appear as applied to him prior to his condemnation as an heretic; and, moreover, the various ways in which it is written, *e.g.*, sometimes Valdo, sometimes Valdus, at other times Valdesius or Valdensis, shows that the word was not a proper name, but a mere appellative. So with regard to the idea that Vaudois comes from Vaudes, a sorcerer, it would be more correct to say that the term sorcerer was one applied by the inhabitants of the plains to those who were Vaudois, or hill-men, under the notion that the inhabitants of such localities practised sorcery. Hence we are compelled to assume that the name is purely geographical, and applied from time immemorial to the persons living in those valleys of Piedmont which have ever formed part of the Italian territory, and are not to be confounded with the Swiss Canton de Vaud, bearing a name so like because of the similarity of geographical conformation.

In answer to the next question, How long have the Waldenses lived in the locality from which they derive their name? *Da ogni tempo, da tempo immemoriale*—from all time, from time immemorial—is the claim set up by them in their earliest documents, and repeated over and over again in their petitions to the House of Savoy for liberty of conscience.[A] Nor is there any attempt to refute this claim of antiquity on the part of their princes or their persecutors.

To this statement of the Waldenses themselves we will add corroborative testimony from others.

Their enemies. We begin with Reinerius the Inquisitor, A.D. 1250. He refers to the Waldenses under the term of Leonists, and says that this sect has been of longer continuance (than the others to which he refers), having lasted, some say, from the time of Pope Sylvester (314), and others from the time of the apostles.

Pilichdorf, a writer of the same date, expressly asserts that the Waldenses claimed to have existed from the time of Pope Sylvester, and Claude Seyssel, Archbishop of Turin from the close of the fifteenth century to the beginning of the sixteenth, and whose diocese extended to the valleys of Piedmont, says that the Waldenses took their origin from Leo, a person in the time of ye Emperor Constantine, who, hating the avarice of Pope Sylvester and the immoderate endowment of the Church of Rome, seceded from her communion, and "*drew after him all who entertained right sentiments about the Christian religion.*"

Next in order we may take the testimony of Rorenco, Grand Prior of St. Roch in Turin, and one of the lords of the valley of Luserne. He was commissioned to investigate the history of the "men of the valleys," and published the result of his labours in the year 1632. He says "that the Waldenses were no new sect, but had been in those valleys for more than five or six centuries," and in proof of this remarks further, that "no edict of any prince who gave permission for the introduction of this religion into these parts can be found. Princes only give permission to their subjects to continue in the religion of their ancestors." Cassini, an Italian priest, declares that the tradition handed down was, that "the Waldenses were as ancient as the Christian Church."

Another writer, Henri de Corvie, describes them as men descended from "an ancient race, inhabiting the Alps, and have been always attached to ancient customs." Voltaire, an impartial witness, speaks of the Waldenses as "the remains of the first Christians of Gaul." If it be asked for documentary proof, in the possession of the Waldensians themselves, it should be remembered that Leger, the historian, collected together all that he could find, and that these were taken from him when he was imprisoned in Turin, A.D. 1655. Still, documents of great value and antiquity have been preserved, and among these must be enumerated "The Noble Lesson," a didactic poem of about five hundred lines. Three MSS. of this poem are preserved in the libraries of the Universities of Cambridge, Geneva, and Dublin, and the date assigned is *early* in the twelfth century. The dialect in which it is written is also considered by some as an unquestionable proof of the high antiquity of the document. For example, the eminent philologist, M. Renouard, writing as a philologist, and not as an historian, remarks that "*the dialect of the Vaudois is an idiom intermediate between the decomposition of the language of the Romans and the establishment of a new grammatical system.*" This philological circumstance shows the extreme earliness of the period at which the Waldenses must have betaken themselves to the Cottian Alps, inasmuch as it proves that they left the Italian plains before the establishment of the new grammatical system referred to by M. Renouard. This is the opinion of Mr. Faber, who contends that "the primevally Latin Vaudois must have retired from the lowlands of Italy to the valleys of Piedmont in the very days of primitive Christianity, and *before* the breaking up of the Roman empire by the incursions of the Teutonic nations." And this leads to another question. Why did these people leave their homes in the fertile plains and betake themselves to the less temperate climate and the rugged soil of a mountainous region? Plainly there must have been some very urgent cause, and that cause may be readily perceived in the record of the persecutions against the Christians under the Pagan emperors during the second, third, and fourth centuries.

FOOTNOTES:

[A] E.G.—In a memorial to Philibert Emmanuel, A.D. 1559, they say, "This religion which we profess is not only ours ... but it was the religion of our fathers, grandfathers, great-grandfathers, and other yet more ancient predecessors of ours, and of the blessed martyrs, confessors, prophets, and apostles; *and if any can prove the contrary, we are ready to subscribe and yield thereunto.*"

CHAPTER IV.

We come now to the creed and organization of the Waldensian Church. First, as regards the rule of faith, it expresses its belief in the supremacy of the Word of God in terms precisely identical with the Sixth Article of the Church of England. And, in a document previously referred to, declares, "We do protest before the Almighty and All-just God, before whose tribunal we must all one day appear, that we intend to live and die in the holy faith, piety, and religion of our Lord Jesus Christ; and that we do abhor all heresies that have been and are condemned by the Word of God.

"We do embrace the most holy doctrine of the prophets and apostles, as likewise of the Nicene and Athanasian Creeds. We subscribe to the four councils, and to all the ancient fathers, in all such things as are not repugnant to the analogy of faith." They protest against the assumptions and the encroachments of the papacy much in the same way as do the Thirty-nine Articles of the Church of England; they also accept the opinions of evangelical Christendom in relation to the fall of man—justification by faith alone; redemption through the merits of the lord Jesus Christ; regeneration by the Holy Spirit; fruitfulness in good works as the necessary result of a living faith; the character of worship acceptable to God; the obligations and privileges of the Lord's day, and of the two sacraments, baptism and the Lord's Supper, as appointed by the Lord Jesus Christ, and binding upon the grateful observance of His believing people. It is not true, as has sometimes been asserted, that they have ever rejected the practice of infant baptism. They have prepared and enjoined the use of a very sound and full catechism, in which the children of the Waldenses are carefully instructed previous to their admission to the Lord's table.

So far we have sketched the leading points in the creed of the Waldensian Church. We now come to its organization. There seem to have been three epochs, so to speak, in reference to this feature of its history. For some eleven hundred years it remained as a portion of the universal and primitive church, rejecting the encroachments of the papal power, and the corruptions of Christian doctrine which that power imposed, not by authoritative enactments so much as by irregular influences, upon the greater part of the Western Church. During this time the church in the valleys of Piedmont retained that system of church government and worship which had been accepted by most, if not all, sections of the Christian Church in the third and fourth centuries. It was, therefore, during this period that the Waldensian Church enjoyed the privilege of that episcopacy which she never rejected as a matter of principle, but became deprived of by circumstances which gave her no choice. In proof of this I refer to that passage in the letter of Jerome to Riparius respecting Vigilantius, whose zealous and persevering opposition to the worship of saints, images, and relics, &c., had greatly provoked the irascible monk of Bethlehem. "I saw (says Jerome) a short time ago that monster Vigilantius. I would fain have bound this madman by passages of Holy Writ, as Hippocrates advises to confine maniacs with bonds; but he has departed, he has withdrawn, he has hurried away, he has escaped, and from the space between the Alps, *where Cottius reigned*,[B] and the waves of the Adriatic, his cries have reached me. Oh, infamous! he has found *even among the bishops* accomplices of his wickedness."

Here then we learn that in the country inhabited by the Waldenses there were bishops opposing the corruption and contending for the priests of the Christian faith. Nor was this confined even to Northern Italy; for we learn that two centuries later Gregory the Great, who was pope from A.D. 590 to 604, censures Seremius, bishop of Marseilles, for not only forbidding the adoration of images (which Gregory says he would have commended), but for actually destroying the images themselves. Towards the middle of the eighth century the prelates of the Gallican Church especially distinguished themselves by their determined opposition to such doctrines as the worship of images and relics, masses for the dead, purgatory, celibacy of the priests, supremacy of the popes, &c., errors inculcated, it would seem, by the English monk Boniface, who has been called the apostle of Germany.

The correspondence between Pope Zachary and Boniface further reveals the existence of a Christian community in Germany, holding a faith more evangelical, and observing a ritual more scriptural, than that which Rome was seeking to impose; *e.g.*, Zachary says in his tenth letter: "As for the priests, whom your fraternity report to have found (who are more numerous than the Catholics (*sic*) wandering about disguised under the name of bishops or priests, not ordained by Catholic (*i.e.*, Romish) bishops, who deceive the people) ... they are false vagabonds," &c.

But the most interesting proof of the existence of evangelical resistance to popish corruption is that afforded by the conduct of Claude, bishop of the metropolitical see of Turin, and in such close proximity to those valleys whose history we are considering.

Claude, bishop of Turin, was a native of Spain, and so incidentally brings to mind the remembrance of the fact that Spain, too, had upon her soil in days gone by those who loved "to worship God in sincerity and truth." He was chosen by Louis the Meek for the bishopric of Turin, on the ground of his scriptural piety and evangelical eloquence. Being attacked by Jonas, bishop of Orleans, and others, he defended himself with great ability; and in reply to the charge that he was seeking to establish a new sect, he answers, "I, who remain in the unity of the Church, and proclaim the truth, aim at forming no new sect; but, as far as lies in my power, *I repress sects*, schisms, superstitions, and heresies; I have combated, overthrown, and crushed them, and, by God's assistance, I shall not cease to do so to the utmost." These words of Claude, "I repress sects," seem clearly to imply that in the diocese of Turin disaffection to Romish innovation had a recognized existence, and definite, though not of necessity an independent, organization; and that Claude, standing firm upon the platform "of the faith once delivered to the saints" as the true centre of unity, was attaching to himself all those whose principles were analogous to the ancient church of the valleys. And I think we may fairly assume that the fifteen years' episcopate of so distinguished a prelate must have given a great assistance to that portion of his people who sought "to stand in the old ways." Indeed the Marquis de Beauregard, in his *Historic Memoirs*, expressly states that this bishop had a great number of adherents, that they were anathematized by the pope, persecuted by the lay princes, chased from the open country, and *so forced to take refuge in the mountains*, where they have kept their ground from that time, always checked, but always endeavouring to extend themselves. (Vol. ii. p. 50.)

After the time of Claude, however, the connection of the church in the valleys with that to which it originally belonged became probably less and less distinct, owing to the more decided growth of corruption and the extension of papal influence, so that, as regards the greater portion of Europe, primitive faith and practice was submerged by papal superstition and tyranny. Therefore about this time, as appears from the Waldensian book entitled *Antichrist*, the church of the valleys entered on what we call its second epoch, and became isolated as regards organization, though not as regards doctrine, from the earlier church. This epoch may be regarded as reaching down to about the seventeenth century. I fix upon this date because of the remarkable providence which befell the Vaudois Church in 1630.

This was none other than a pestilential visitation brought into the valleys by the French troops, who were at this time occupying the valleys. By this terrible plague some ten thousand of the Vaudois perished, including twelve pastors. Only three pastors being now left, application was made to Geneva for assistance, and pastors being sent from thence introduced a polity which was Presbyterian rather than Episcopalian. Still the marked deference to authority, the succession of the ministers elected by their predecessors from time to time, the orderly administration of the sacraments, the use of the creeds and of a liturgy, the entire absence of any protest against the orders of the ministry customary in the early church, while so much is so pointedly said respecting corruptions of doctrine, clearly sustain the inference that the Waldensian Church adapted herself to the form of organization adopted by the reformed churches of the continent not from choice, but from such a concurrence of circumstances as completely vindicates her from any wilful departure from the traditions of her earlier history.

It was at this time also, and from the circumstance that the pastors supplied from Geneva could only officiate in the French tongue, that the French language was used in worship.

This brings me to notice the organization of the Waldensian Church as it now exists, and has existed for the last two hundred years. The full and formal confession of faith is that which was agreed upon by the synod of 1655, and confirmed in the years 1839 and 1855.

The Evangelical Waldensian Church, in its widest sense, embraces all those churches whom God in His mercy has condescended to preserve from time immemorial, and subject to numberless persecutions in the valleys of the Italian Alps. It also includes those churches which have been more recently added. As regards organization, the Waldensian is subdivided into parishes, and is governed by means of a general assembly of the parish, a consistory, synod, and table.

The general assembly of the parish is composed of all the members of the church, being men who are twenty-five years of age. To this assembly belongs (*a*) the nomination of the pastors; (*b*) the deputies to synod; (*c*) the elders and deacons; (*d*) the initiative of any proposal for altering the constitution of the church.

It is always presided over by the pastor, or, in his unavoidable absence, by a member of the consistory chosen for the purpose.

The Consistory is composed of the pastor, who presides, the elders, and the deacons, the last of whom have only a deliberative vote. Its functions are to provide for the spiritual wants of the parish, and also the poor and sick; to assist in the distribution of the elements at the administration of the Holy Communion; to nominate the teachers and superintend the schools, either wholly or in association with the communal council; also to administer church discipline; distribute parochial charities and funds for religious purposes. On this behalf each consistory appoints its own treasurer.

The Synod is the representative assembly of the Vaudois Church, and consists of all recognized pastors and certain laymen chosen by the parishes. It takes cognizance of every matter affecting the welfare and duties of the church; it alters, adds, or abolishes all rules and regulations connected with its administration or discipline; it directs the course of theological study and admission to the ministry; it nominates the members of the table or any special bodies of commissioners for particular occasions; it superintends all evangelic work, whether in the valleys or its numerous mission stations in other places. It now meets yearly, but in former times its meetings were seldom, and were attended by a representative of the civil power.

THE TABLE is the executive of the Vaudois Church, and consists of five members, the moderator, assistant moderator, and secretary being pastors, with two laymen. The table is appointed by the synod from year to year, and responsible to that body in respect of its operations.

The officers of the Vaudois Church are pastors, evangelists, elders, and deacons. To exercise the office of pastor a person must be set apart by the laying on of hands, previous to which he must (α) have attained the age of twenty-three, (β) have the requisite gifts for the work of the ministry, (γ) be of irreproachable character, (δ) receive a certificate from his university or other place of education, (ϵ) profess convictions in harmony with the doctrines and discipline of the Vaudois Church. These points are decided by the table, in concert with the whole body of the pastors of the church. Furthermore, a pastor is not allowed to have the sole care of a parish before he has reached the age of twenty-five years.

It is not necessary to speak of the functions of the evangelists, as the name itself is explicit, and the office one common to all evangelical churches, although denominated by a different title, *e.g.* catechist, reader, lay missionary.

The elders are lay members of the church of well-known religious character, residing in the parish, and not receiving any benefit from the funds they may be called upon to administer. At an election of an elder for the first time he is required before installation to undergo an examination by a commission from the consistory of his own parish, assisted by a pastor from the nearest adjoining parish. The elder is chosen for life, unless he voluntarily resigns, or falls into a breach of church discipline, or becomes incapacitated by failing health; in the latter case, however, he retains the title of honorary elder.

The deacons must have much the same qualifications as the elders. They are elected for five years, and their special work is the care of the sick and needy. In addition to a zealous observance of the Lord's-day, the Waldensian Church pays a religious regard to Christmas-day, New-year's-day, Ascension-day, and Good Friday, which last it keeps with great solemnity as a fast-day common to the whole Church of Christ.

FOOTNOTES:

[B] The Cottian Alps are to the north of Mount Viso, and among them are the valleys of the Waldenses.

CHAPTER V.

THE BEGINNING OF PAPAL PERSECUTIONS.

"We kept Thy faith 'gainst kings of might,
And potentates infernal;
We kept Thy faith in Rome's despite,
By help of grace supernal.
The foe was fierce, the war was long;
But oh! our helper was more strong,Our lover was eternal."

During the struggles of the papacy for temporal aggrandizement and political usurpation, which marked its character from the seventh to the twelfth centuries, anything so religious as even the attempt to convert heretics by fire and sword seems little attended to. But in the twelfth century arose the epoch in which men were to be thrown into a burning fiery furnace who would not bow down to the tyranny of him who sat enthroned in the city of the seven hills. Otho IV., Emperor of Germany by favour of the pope, first gave his sanction to the persecution of the Waldenses, at the instigation of James, bishop of Turin, about the end of the 12th century.[C] But the first *systematic* persecution began under the regency exercised by Yolande, widow of Amadeus IX., Duke of Savoy, A.D. 1475. The expression (in her directions to the governors of Pinerolo, Cavour, and the magistrate at Lucerna), "It is our pleasure that the inhabitants of the valley of Lucerna especially may be able *to enter* into the bosom of the holy mother church," would seem to recognize the fact that the Vaudois were a community independent of Rome, otherwise we should expect the word return, which is so generally used in reference to heretics, as the Church of Rome delights to stigmatize all who reject her sway. This edict of Yolande led to the martyrdom of Vaudois pastors, some by fire, some by hanging, some in ways more revolting and excruciating, at Turin and other places. But the destruction of a few victims would not satisfy the malignant spirit of the papal antichrist, therefore the work of persecution must be organized on a larger scale. Innocent VIII. selected Albert de Capitaneis, Archdeacon of Cremona, as his agent for the accomplishment of this pious design.

"One of the saintly murderous brood,
To carnage and the crosier given,
Who think through unbelievers' blood
Lies their directest path to heaven."

(MOORE, slightly altered.)

The papal bull initiating this work of shame promised to all who should engage in it "plenary indulgence, with remission of their sins once and at the hour of death." It also gave permission to appropriate the lands and goods of the heretics. All along the valley of the Po, and over the regions of the Cottian Alps, the bull of Innocent was talked of. Charles VIII. of France and Charles II. of Savoy sanctioned its design. The year 1488 marks an era of suffering for the Vaudois and of infamy to Rome.

Some 18,000 soldiers responded to the call of De Capitaneis. He forms them into two bodies. One proceeds to devastate Dauphine and the district near from the west, while the other division, attacking from Piedmont, is to ravage the east; and as the two bodies approach each other they aim to enclose their victims, and so to prevent their escape. These victims were all unprepared for the vengeance which impended. Engaged in peaceful tillage, they had no means of defence, but fled to the rocks and caves, where their persecutors followed them, and being unable to reach them in their retreats, they piled up fuel at the mouths of the caverns, and so compelled the Vaudois to choose between death by suffocation or the sword.

By such conduct some 3000 persons, including 400 young children, perished in the vale of Loyse. The Val Pragela also suffered much. But in the Clusone, after the first feelings of surprise had passed away, the inhabitants successfully repulsed their invaders. In the valley of Lucerna, San Giovanni, La Torre, Villaro Bobbio, and their hamlets, fell into the hands of the enemy. Still their career was sometimes checked by successful resistance, and deserved retribution. An example of this occurred to a detachment numbering some 700 Piedmontese troops, who were attempting to surprise the valley of San Martino by way of the Col Juliano. This body of soldiers, on reaching Pommiers, was attacked with such vigour and determination by the inhabitants of Prali, that only one of their number escaped destruction. This was an ensign, who concealed himself under a mass of snow, which had been excavated by the summer heat. Cold and hunger eventually compelled him to descend and ask mercy from those whom he had come to destroy. His petition was granted, and he was allowed to depart with the news of the defeat and destruction of his companions.

After this humiliating repulse, the invaders sought to attack the vale of Angrogna, as being the heart and centre of the valleys, and the place of refuge and defence to their threatened inhabitants.

Indeed, the Vaudois, unable to contend with the enemy's troops in the plains, had betaken themselves (as many as could) to that natural fortress, the Pra del Torre, which God had provided in the upper part of the Val Angrogna. I shall have much to say about this sacred and glorious spot—the more than a Thermopylæ to these Christian heroes, ennobled by a bravery equal to that of the Spartan, but radiant with brighter memories. But here I only digress to add that the invaders' attempt to get possession of this valley from the heights of Roccamanente were happily frustrated. The Vaudois had to endure a severe contest, for which they prepared themselves by prayer. Their enemies, with their leader, seeing them on their knees, ridiculed their piety and threatened their destruction. But Le Noir of Mondovi, himself having raised his visor on account of the heat, and to show his contempt for his adversaries, was mortally wounded between his eyes by an arrow. His companions were so terrified that they retreated with great loss. The enemy, however, irritated and ashamed, renewed the attack from another position on the side of Rocciaglia. They sought to enter the Pra del Torre by a narrow defile. At this moment a *thick fog* so confused them that they were afraid to move lest they should run into danger. The Angrognians, emboldened by this interposition of Providence, issued forth from their retreats, and by means of their knowledge of the locality cut off the escape of their enemies, and forced them over the precipitous rocks into the foaming torrent, where large numbers perished, including a man of gigantic size named Saquet, whose eventful death has caused the pool in which he fell to be called Tompi Saquet.

After similar attempts in other parts of the valleys, during which time much blood was shed, this first of the great persecutions, which had lasted a year, ended in 1489, by Charles II., Prince of Piedmont and Duke of Savoy, who felt ashamed of the cruelties which were inflicted.

FOOTNOTES:

[C] Monastier gives some very interesting information on the persecution of the Vaudois out of Piedmont (chap. xiv.), which lies beyond the scope of this volume.

CHAPTER VI.

Although the story of the long-continued and heroically endured sufferings of the Vaudois may have been the most prominent thought in the minds of those who recall their history, yet it is at least to the Christian as important to remember their works of faith and labours of love in the cause of Christ. Indeed were it not for the latter we should never have known the former. It would seem as if the missionary zeal of the Waldenses was one of the chief causes (or at least occasions) of the persecutions which they endured. Hence Bernard de Foucald (*Monastier History*), a writer of the twelfth century, says, "These Waldenses, although condemned by Pope Lucius II., continued to pour forth, with daring effrontery, far and wide all over the world, the poison of their perfidy."

Indeed a church whose motto was a burning torch, and whose directory that sacred word which counsels the followers of Christ to "let their light shine before men," was not likely to be content with possessing the truth merely for itself. So we learn that in the distribution of the funds contributed by the church a portion was assigned to the purpose of maintaining a body of pastors for the foreign work. These pastors being trained and set apart by the barbes for the work of the ministry were named by the synod for their special sphere of labour. The work of preparation for the ministry involved the learning by heart of the first and fourth gospels, the whole of the canonical epistles, and a large portion of the Old Testament. The missionaries to foreign churches generally remained abroad for two years. Although this work was one of danger, no reluctance to undertake it was evinced. This shows the power of the gospel in their hearts, as well as the deference shown by the younger pastors to their seniors in the ministry of the Word and sacraments. As a rule it would seem that the synod despatched their missionaries two and two. Thus, following the example of the great Head of the Church, and providing for the necessities of the times, one of the two was selected as more or less acquainted with the character of the places and persons they were about to visit.

The mode in which the Waldensian missionaries laboured illustrated at times the wisdom of the serpent as well as the harmlessness of the dove; *e.g.*, they obtained access to the higher classes in the character of pedlars. Having displayed their goods, chiefly of an ornamental kind, and a purchase had been concluded, if the pedlar were asked, "Have you anything else for sale?" he would reply, "I have jewels far more precious than these, and if you will not betray me to the clergy I will make you a present of them." Being answered satisfactorily on this point, he would proceed to say, "I have a pearl so brilliant that by means of it one may learn to know God; I have another so splendid that it kindles the love of God in the heart of him who possesses it." And then he would proceed to quote various portions of Scripture.

The following verses from a modern poet happily describes one of these incidents—

"'O, lady fair! I have yet a gem,
Which a purer lustre flings
Than the diamond flash of the jewelled crown
On the lofty brow of kings;
A wonderful pearl of exceeding price,
Whose virtue shall not decay;
Whose light shall be as a spell to thee,
And a blessing on thy way.'

"The lady glanced at the mirroring steel,
Where her youthful form was seen,
Where her eyes shone clear, and her dark locks waved
Their clasping pearls between;
'Bring forth thy pearl of exceeding worth,
Thou traveller grey and old;
And name the price of thy precious gem,
And my pages shall count thy gold.'

"The cloud went off from the pilgrim's brow,
As a small and meagre book,
Unchased with gold or diamond gem,
From his folding robe he took:
'Here, lady fair, is the pearl of price;
May it prove as such to thee!
Nay, keep thy gold—I ask it not—
FOR THE WORD OF GOD IS FREE.'

"The hoary traveller went his way,
But the gift he left behind
Hath had its pure and perfect work
On that high-born maiden's mind;
And she hath turned from her pride of sin
To the lowliness of truth,
And given her human heart to God
In its beautiful hour of youth.

"And she hath left the old grey walls,
Where an evil faith hath power,

The courtly knights of her father's train,
And the maidens of her bower;
And she hath gone to the Vaudois Vale,
By lordly feet untrod,
Where the poor and needy of earth are rich
In the perfect love of God!"

But another mode of spreading the gospel in distant parts was by colonizing. This measure was forced upon the Waldenses by the cruelties to which they were exposed in the South of France. Their earliest colonies (A.D. 1340) were at Apulia and Calabria, and in Liguria. The lords of the soil in Southern Italy permitted them to settle on favourable terms. They built several towns, such as Oltromontani, grew in temporal prosperity, and lived in peace for many years. As regards ecclesiastical matters, they maintained direct communion with their brethren in the valleys, who supplied them with pastors. These pastors, in their journeys backwards and forwards, visited their faithful brethren scattered throughout Italy. The barbes, indeed, possessed a house in each of the cities of Florence, Genoa, and Venice. As regards numbers, it is not unlikely that the Waldenses in Italy, France, and Germany at this time (the close of the fourteenth century) were about eight hundred thousand. Venice alone contained six thousand Vaudois, it is said, at this time. But this state of external peacefulness continued only for a time. The very superiority of the Vaudois to their neighbours attracted attention to their religious peculiarities. The Romish clergy complained "that they did not live like other people in matters of religion; that they made none of their children priests or nuns; that they did not concern themselves about chants, wax tapers, lights, bells, or even masses for the dead; that they had no images in their temples," &c. All this criticism was intensified by the news of that great reformation of the sixteenth century, which awakened alike the fears and the rage of Rome, and sent forth her legionaries everywhere like blood-hounds keenly on the scent for the tracks of heresy.

They were not long before they met with the evidences of a purer faith than that of the pope's in the sunny regions south of the Tiber. The Waldenses in Calabria had heard of the revived faith and growing zeal of their brethren in Piedmont. They determined, like them, to lay aside all concealment of their religious profession, and openly to proclaim their heart-deep convictions as to the vital principles of the gospel of Christ. As a means of a higher and truer confession of Christ, they sought a colleague for their pastor, Etienne Négrin (who was from the valleys), from Geneva. A young Piedmontese, Jean Louis Pascal, was just then finishing his studies at Lausanne. Brought up as a papist and a soldier, he renounced his former creed and profession for that of the gospel of Christ. Nor was it without cost of another kind he undertook the perilous work of the ministry in Calabria. He was engaged in marriage to Camilla Guerina, and in setting out for Italy (though unconsciously to themselves, perhaps) they parted for ever as regards this world.

His ministry was greatly blessed in Calabria. The light so often placed under a bushel was elevated conspicuously by the candlestick of his labours. But while believers rejoiced, superstitious bigots raved. The Marquis Spinello, chief proprietor in the Vaudois colony, alarmed for his credit with the clergy, and contrary to his former kindness, sends for the principal offenders, including the pastor and his friend, Marco Uscegli. The two latter were cast into prison, and the former dismissed with threatenings. This happened about 1558 or 1559, and was followed by more determined measures of the bishop of the diocese and the pope. The latter deputed Cardinal Alexandrin, inquisitor general, to extirpate heresy in the kingdom of Naples. All attempts failing to induce attendance at mass, they were pursued by soldiers, and obliged to make an armed resistance, which led to the flight of their assailants. After a few days the Vaudois, who had fled to the woods, were hunted by dogs. Nearly all were captured or killed on the spot. Those captured were tortured in the most horrible way to extort confessions of misdeeds which their enemies had fabricated. One Bernard Conte, who had thrown away a crucifix forced into his hands, was daubed with pitch, and then set on fire. Their sufferings are too many and revolting to recount. Let it suffice to add that the bodies of the victims were so numerous as to line the roads for a distance of thirty-six miles, being placed on stakes for that purpose from Montalto to Chateau-Vilar. The pastor, Etienne Négrin, was either tortured or starved to death. But Pascal was reserved for a more public immolation. On the 9th of September, 1560, an immense crowd assembled in the courtyard of the castle of St. Angelo. A scaffold had been erected close by with a pile of faggots. A stage with seats furnished suitably for the use of the pope, Pius IV., his cardinals, and ecclesiastics of all ranks, was placed near. When the martyr reached the scaffold he declared to the people that he was put to death for no crime but that of confessing with boldness his Master and Saviour Jesus Christ. "As to those who hold the pope to be God upon earth and vicar of Jesus Christ," he said, "they are strangely mistaken, seeing that in everything he shows himself to be a mortal enemy of Christ's doctrine and service." He was then put to death, but not before he had "made the pope and his cardinals gnash their teeth." In this way the Waldenses were driven out of Calabria, at a time, let it be remembered, when in the gracious providence of God the Reformation was being firmly established in England.

We pass on then to consider what was the condition of the Vaudois in their own valleys after the termination of their sufferings narrated in the fifth chapter. We have glanced at the revival of true religion in the valleys and Vaudois colonies. Suffice it, then, to add that the sympathy shown by Farel (present at the Synod of Angrogna, 1532), Ecomlapadius, Bucer, and others, all served to encourage the reviving zeal of that church which had so long held aloft the standard of God's truth, though at times it may be somewhat weary with the strife and burden involved in that high distinction of witnessing for Christ in a world that either forgot or denied Him. One of the signs of the earnestness which characterized the Vaudois Church at this time was the translation of the Holy Scriptures into French (for the benefit of the reformed churches) out of the Romaunce dialect, in which the Vaudois had possessed the word of God from time immemorial. A further proof of piety was shown in the erection of buildings for public worship, A.D. 1535. The first temple was at St. Lorenzo, near Chamforans, the site of the Angrogna Synod; and a second was built at Serre, in the same valley. This latter temple was standing at the time of our visit, though needing repair. It would seem that the evangelical spirit was so decided at this period that the few priests who continued hovering about the valleys in the hope of effecting perversions retired in despair. The process of church building went on, so that in 1556 several temples existed in the Val Lucerna and San Martino. But such a state of things was not permitted to continue without fresh opposition. In the year 1556 the Pope and Henry II. of France give orders to the parliament of Turin to repress these heretical movements. They send out two of their body, who visit the valley of San Martino, and publish an edict threatening all who refuse obedience to its commands. They summoned before them a labourer, and asked him why he had taken his child for baptism to the temple at Angrogna? He replied, "Because baptism was there administered according to the institution of Jesus Christ." The same man, on being commanded to have his child re-baptized, asked for permission to pray before he gave his answer. Having done this, he asked the magistrate to give him a paper assuming the responsibility and the sin of the transaction. This demand so embarrassed his persecutor that he was discharged without further molestation. A noble representative, however, of the class of pedlars of which we have spoken before did not so easily escape his persecutors. This devoted Christian, Barthélemi Hector, of Poictiers, visited from place to place with copies of the word of God, which he read to the people at their work, and sold to those who could buy. On this errand of mercy he betook himself to the slopes of that mountain (La Vachere) which overlook the Pra del Tor. The eagle of the Romish inquisitors tracked him on his rounds, and carried him to Turin that he might answer for so foul a crime! His judges addressed him in the following strain: "You have been surprised in the act of selling heretical books." He responded with the courage of one who knew in whom he believed. "If the Bible contains heresies for you, it is *truth for me*!" But, replied the judges, "You use the Bible to keep men from going to mass." "If the Bible keeps men from the mass it proves that God condemns it as idolatry," he replied; and when further called upon to retract, he asked, with holy dignity, "Can I change truth as if it were a garment?" Such courage and skill in defending his position impressed his judges, and they hoped, by long delay and promises of pardon, to shake his firmness. But he was upheld by the grace so richly vouchsafed, and he died exclaiming, "Glory to God that He judges me worthy of death for Him." This martyrdom was followed, about two years later, by two other remarkable cases. The first was a young student educated by the republic of Berne, named Nicolas Sartoire. He was returning for a few weeks' holiday to his native land, and had scarcely crossed the frontier of Piedmont when, resisting all temptations to deny his faith, he was burnt at Aosta, on the 4th of May, 1557.

The second, Geoffrey Varaille, was a man of fifty, *the son of one of those who had taken part in the persecution of 1488.*

While following his duties as a monk, he was convinced of the errors of popery, and after a period of study received ordination, and became pastor of San Giovanni in 1557. He was waylaid while on a visit to Busca, his native place, and carried to Turin, where he made a noble confession of his faith amidst the flames on the 29th of March, 1558. Other victims would have been sacrificed had not the Protestant princes of Germany and the evangelical cantons of Switzerland intervened, and so for a little longer the church in the valleys had a measure of rest prior to the outburst of another fierce attack.

CHAPTER VII.

The death of Mary Queen of England put out the fires of persecution in our own beloved land; but, alas! served to rekindle them in the devoted valleys of the Alps. By the treaty of Cambresis, 1559, the kings of France and Spain bound themselves anew to the extirpation of heresy. Moreover, they agreed that the conquests made by each country during the preceding eight years should be restored. Thus all the gains of Francis I. and Henry II. of France were given up, and Philibert Emmanuel of Savoy was transposed by a scratch of the pen from the condition of a landless mercenary into that of a sovereign prince. Would that he had been free to rule as his own disposition and that of his evangelical consort, Margaret of Navarre, would have prompted! But the provisions of the treaty bound him to persecute rather than protect his loyal subjects in the valleys. Too soon the evidences of this appeared. First came edicts forbidding any one to attend non-Catholic preaching. Then commands to hear mass. After that were kindled the fires in which many bravely endured the worst rather than abjure the faith. These proceedings were, however, preliminary to an attack on the valleys. So the Vaudois betake themselves to united prayer for guidance. After deliberation it was resolved to address the duke, the duchess, and the council of the state. In these addresses they set forth the antiquity of their religion, the conformity of their belief with the creeds and four first councils of the church, and the writings of the early fathers, and vindicate themselves from the calumnies of their enemies, also protesting their loyalty to their prince. After much difficulty these documents reached the parties addressed, but owing to the interference of the pope nothing satisfactory was gained. The monks of Pinerolo signalized themselves by the ardour with which they harassed the Vaudois. They employed large numbers of vile characters as mercenaries to make incursions into the valleys. On one occasion they secured possession of a pastor by treachery. Having alarmed his parishioners, they attempted his rescue. Some of these were slain at once by the ruffians from the abbey, others were captured, and by a refinement of cruelty (such as the Church of Rome surpasses all her competitors in) were made, especially the women, to carry the faggots for the fire which was to burn their beloved minister. Occasionally these frocked and sandalled ruffians met with deserved retribution at the hands of those whose homes they desolated. But these things were but the distant rumbling of the tempest, which ere long would burst upon the faithful Christians of the Alps. Their leaders foresaw what was coming, and before the army of persecution actually invaded their soil, they strengthened themselves by praise and prayer, by the word of God, and the ordinance of the Lord's Supper.

Thus "strengthening each other's hand in God," they waited the progress of the soldiers. These numbered over four thousand, commanded by the Count de la Trinité. Twelve hundred of them first attacked the heights of Angrogna, and although the defenders numbered but one in six of their assailants, yet they are repulsed with a loss of sixty dead, while the Vaudois only lost three. Other attacks were equally unsuccessful, and so La Trinité persuades the Angrognians to a truce by which they are powerless to resist, although he still continues his own plans of devastation, plunder, and confiscation. Those cruelties drive the people of La Torre to caves and rocks, although it is winter. An instance of cruelty may be narrated in the case of a man aged a hundred and three, who was found by the soldiers hidden in a cave under the guardianship of his granddaughter, a maiden of seventeen. After taking the life of the venerable man, they seek to dishonour the girl, who, preferring death, leaped over the precipice into the stream below. As she did so, tradition says she sang one of their hymns, and that its melody even now floats in the air of those mountain regions, and is heard by the shepherd as he pastures his flock on the slopes of the Vandalin by "the Maiden's Rock." La Trinité continued his persecutions during a period of fifteen months. The Vaudois organized themselves successfully, and were favoured with remarkable deliverances, which we shall refer to more appropriately in a later chapter, as they were chiefly connected with the Pra del Tor. We may, however, state here that some of the most decisive triumphs against the enemy were obtained by means of a troop of one hundred picked marksmen, called "the flying company," because their services were available in all places according to the varying emergencies of their situation. A treaty of peace so nearly approximating to justice as to be denounced by the pope as "a pernicious example," and by a "liberal" Roman Catholic historian[D] as "a blameable weakness," was concluded at Cavour on the 5th of June, 1561, and honourably fulfilled by Philibert Emmanuel to the end of his days, although the Vaudois were still to bear the cross of their Master. The first hardship coming upon them was that of hunger, thirst, and homelessness. Their joy at the departure of the men of war was sadly diminished by the sight of their ruined homes and devastated vineyards and fields. Alas! for them no fig tree could bloom, no vine yield its fruit. The flock had been cut off from the fold, and the herd driven from the stall. The fields could yield no meat, and the time for sowing was past. To add to those disasters, their poor brethren, flying from Calabria naked and destitute, were seeking shelter and nourishment at their hands. Mercifully, however, sympathizing hearts in Germany and Switzerland, nobly led by the Elector Palatine, the Duke of Wurtemburg, the Marquis of Baden, the energy of Calvin, and seconded by the churches of Strasbourg and Provence, supplied their great distress.

Persecution was renewed by indirect means. Castrocaro, forgetful of the kindness showed him during the late war, when he was taken prisoner by the

Vaudois while fighting against them, undertook the task of harassing the valleys. He occupied the castle at La Torre. He ill-treated many of the pastors, especially Gilles. He built the fort at Miraboc, tried to prevent the meetings of the synods, &c. Large numbers had again to choose between the idolatrous mass or the dungeon unless they betook themselves to flight.

It was at this time that the Elector Palatine wrote a remonstrance which deserves to be perpetuated out of regard both to its own merits and those of the noble writer. Addressing the Duke of Savoy, he said, "Let your highness know that there is a God in heaven ... from whom nothing is hid. Let your highness take care not voluntarily to make war upon God, and not to persecute Christ in the person of His members; for if He permit this for a time in order to exercise the patience of His people, He will nevertheless at last chastise the persecutors by horrible punishments. Let not your highness be misled by the seducing discourses of the papists, who, perhaps, will promise you the kingdom of heaven and eternal life, provided ... you exterminate these Huguenots, as they now call good Christians; for assuredly no one can enter the kingdom of heaven by cruelty, inhumanity, and calumny." He also points to the folly of persecution by reminding him that "the ashes of the martyrs are the seed of the Church;" and further, "that the Christian religion was established by persuasion and not by violence, ... that it is nothing else than a firm and enlightened persuasion of God, and of His will, as revealed in His Word and engraven in the hearts of believers by the Holy Spirit; it cannot when once rooted be torn away by tortures," &c.

It is probable that the effect of so plain and forcible a remonstrance helped to protect the Vaudois of Piedmont from the horrible cruelties which befell their brethren in France during the infamous massacre of St. Bartholomew. On the 19th of October, 1574, died the good Duchess of Savoy, Margaret of France, who had been the courageous and faithful friend of her husband's Protestant subjects. Shortly after her death Castrocaro, like another zealous persecutor of the Waldenses under La Trinité, Charles Truchet, perished ignominiously; the former by his own sword, taken from him by his adversaries; the latter in prison, deserted by those whose willing tool he had been in deeds of blood! Philibert Emmanuel was succeeded by his son Charles Emmanuel in 1580. An invasion of the French in 1592 was attempted as the means of prejudicing the new king against his faithful subjects in the valleys, but happily in vain, and he assured them of his gracious disposition in an interview at Villaro. However, the Waldenses were annoyed by the visits of popish missionaries, headed by the Archbishop of Turin. Unable to succeed in open discussions, the monks had recourse to bribing persons of bad character. They also laid claim to tithes, closed the schools, and pursued other forms of oppression. In 1624 they were commanded to destroy the temples in their six communes. And during these years the inquisition ever and anon laid hold of some fresh victim for the dungeon and the stake. A merchant of La Torre, named Coupin, Sebastian Basan, and Louis Malherbe, were added to the noble army of Vaudois martyrs, besides scores who languished and died by secret violence between the years 1601-1626.

The monks renewed their old game of kidnapping the children of the Vaudois. An effort was made to establish convents all through the valleys by Rorenco, prior of Lucerna. The only place they could succeed in was that of La Torre, where evangelical worship was forbidden. After the invasion of the French came the terrible plague in 1630. A brief interval of peace and hope beamed upon the valleys with its smile; but, alas! it was but brief. The restlessness of papal hostility soon awoke to new deeds of cruelty.

Two monks, in the month of May, 1636, appeared in the market-place at La Torre with crucifix in hand, and by their abusive language tried to exasperate the people. And even the noble fidelity of the Vaudois to their young prince, Amadeus II. (only five years of age), at the death of his father, against the attempt of his two uncles, supported by Spain, nor the sufferings they endured at this time from the armies of the uncles, nor the patriotic successes they achieved, seem to have obtained for them anything beyond the most temporary respite. Their temples were again closed. Antonie Leger, pastor of San Giovanni, was obliged to flee for his life. He settled in Geneva as professor of theology and Oriental languages, having lived in the service of the Dutch ambassador at Constantinople many years. And, indeed, things were being put in train for that most furious, perhaps, of all the tempests which the irrepressible pride and cruelty of Rome made to lash its strong rage upon the heads and homes of those whose only fault was—

"They would not leave that precious faith
For Rome's religion, false, impure;
No! no! they rather would endure
To lose their all, yea, even death."

FOOTNOTES:

[D] BOTTA, vol. ii. *Storia d'Italia*.

CHAPTER VIII.

The event to which allusion is made in the close of the foregoing chapter recalls my thoughts and observation, as I stood in the streets of La Torre on what was, as regards the ecclesiastical season, the very anniversary period of that frightful tragedy perpetrated some 214 years before, and remembered still as the "Bloody Pascha." The coincidence seemed to bring home the remembrance of the awful event with a more realizing emphasis. And it was in this train of thought that I cast my eyes upward to the overhanging crag of Castelluzzo. The murderous designs of the edict proclaimed by Gastaldo on the 25th January, 1655; viz., "That all and every one of the heads of families of the pretended reformed religion, of whatever rank or condition, without any exception, both proprietors and inhabitants of the territories of Lucerna, Lucernetta, San Giovanni, La Torre, Bibbiana, Fenile, Campiglione, Bricheariso, and San Secondo, should remove from the aforesaid places within three days to the places allowed by his highness, the names of which places are Bobbio, Villaro, Angrogna, and Rora. Persons contravening the above will incur the penalty of death and confiscation of all their goods, unless within twenty days they declare themselves before us (Gastaldo) to have become Catholics," received its fulfilment by a signal given from this spot on the 24th of April, 1655. The Vaudois had made every submission short of going to mass; but all was in vain, as their extirpation had been determined on by a branch of the inquisition established at Turin in the year 1650. This council was presided over by the Archbishop of Turin, as regards one committee. The Marchioness Pianezza filled the same office over another whose members were ladies! She seems to have breathed the same spirit of ferocity and cunning as that which characterized the conduct of her husband, who commanded the fifteen thousand troops whose gentle entreaties were to win the Vaudois to the orthodoxy of Rome! This army fitly included three regiments of French soldiers, red-handed from the slaughter of the Huguenots; twelve hundred Irish, exiled for their crimes in Ulster; and a number of Piedmontese bandits, attracted by the love of plunder and the promised benedictions of the Church in return for their meritorious labours in extirpating heretics. Two monks led this band of miscreants. One of them, seated on a waggon, brandishing a flaming torch in his left hand and a sword in his right, exhorted the troops to burn and slay. His companion, an aged friar, carried a crucifix before him, exclaiming, "Whoever is a son of the holy church does not pardon heretics; they are the murderers of Christ!" The soldiers, inflamed by these appeals to their fanaticism, went forward with the cry, "Viva la S. Chiesa." They found La Torre deserted; for the people had betaken themselves to the mountains, from whence they could descry the soldiers pillaging their homes. However, they knew that their enemies would not be satisfied with anything less than their lives, and these they resolved to sell as dearly as possible. Pianezza's troops attacked them on the 19th and 20th of April; but the Vaudois on each occasion drove back their assailants with great loss. It was the bravery of the Vaudois at this time that led the Duke of Savoy to say that the skin of a Vaudois cost fifteen or twenty of his best Catholics. Indeed, during this siege fifty of the Piedmontese soldiers were slain by the Vaudois, with only a loss of two by the defenders. The perfidious marquis then resolved to seek by fraud what he was unable to obtain by force.

He invited the deputies—among whom were Leger, the historian and pastor; also the brave Joshua Janavello—to meet him at the convent of La Torre early on Wednesday morning. He represented that he was only in pursuit of those obstinate persons who had resisted the orders of Gastaldo; that the others had nothing to fear, provided they would consent to receive a regiment of infantry and two companies of horse soldiers, *as a mark of obedience and fidelity to their prince*, for two or three days. He then entertained them sumptuously, and sent them back to their communes to persuade their brethren of his sincerity and kindness. Leger and Janavello saw through the trick, but, alas! the others fell into the snare. Accordingly the Vaudois consented to receive the soldiers into their houses and to entertain them as friends. They allowed them to occupy their hiding-places and strongholds, from whence no fair fight had ever driven them. The very eagerness of the soldiers to penetrate into these recesses, and their brutality on their way to the Pra del Tor, opened the eyes of the Vaudois to their miserable condition. It is remarkable that the deputies from Angrogna were the readiest to believe in Pianezza's promises, and also the first to fall victims to his murderous soldiery. On Thursday and Friday Pianezza was occupied with three things—first, in keeping those of the Vaudois on the French frontier from escaping to that country; secondly, in persuading the inhabitants of the valleys of his "good intentions;" and thirdly, resting his soldiers in readiness for the day of slaughter. On Good Friday the Vaudois observed the day according to the usage of their church, by fasting and humiliation. They could not meet in their churches; but in their caverns and mountain dells they cried to the Lord for deliverance from their great distress, and for strength to remain faithful under persecution. The Lord heard their cry; but the church of the valleys was destined to pass through such a sea of suffering, inflicted in the name of the holy Catholic church, as would have made many a pagan persecutor blush with shame. At four o'clock in the morning of Easter-eve, on a signal given from the top of Castelluzzo, Pianezza's troops rose to slaughter the persons under whose roofs they had slept, and of whose food they had partaken the night before. Surely a religion which thus degrades men into monsters should have few apologists in our day. The mind recoils from the enumeration of the horrors of that "bloody Easter." Human depravity, goaded on by every motive which spiritual wickedness could suggest, celebrated such a carnival as must have staggered even a Nero. Men, women, and children were torn limb from limb, after suffering every possible outrage and indecency. Some were rolled from their native rocks to afford merriment to their butchers. Others were impaled on the trees by the wayside. Neither age nor sex hindered this work of brutality; and it is even said that not only did the wretches burn the living bodies of their victims, but also regaled themselves with their flesh, yea, in the presence of their suffering fellows! When these pious soldiers of holy church could no longer slay the Vaudois they burnt their houses and farm buildings, and destroyed their vineyards, with the fruit-trees and other products of the soil.

Nor was Pianezza content with these horrible proceedings at La Torre and its immediate vicinity. On the evening of the same day, Saturday, April 24th, Rora was attacked by five hundred men, the day after by a larger body, the next day by more soldiers still—all in vain. A fourth attack, like the others, was successfully repelled by their noble captain, Janavello, who, with a very small body of helpers, inflicted terrible loss upon the troops, even causing the death of their leader, Mario. These continuous defeats so enraged Pianezza, that he sent them a message to attend mass within twenty-four hours on pain of death. They replied, "We prefer death to the mass a hundred thousand times." On this he assembled a force of ten thousand to attack their village. Janavello fought like a lion, but was overpowered by numbers. His wife and three daughters, with some others, were taken captive. One hundred and twenty-six persons were put to death, and the scenes of the former week were renewed in all their horrible atrocity. The news of this frightful massacre sent a thrill of horror through all that portion of Europe whose sensibilities had not been drugged by the poisonous teaching of the Church of Rome, viz., that heretics are malefactors, and as such may be lawfully exterminated like wild beasts. The representatives of England, Holland, and Switzerland protested against these doings. Cromwell set an example to all rulers, whether kings or presidents. His envoy, Sir Samuel Morland, read a despatch in the presence of Carlo, Emmanuel II., Duke of Savoy, and of his mother, who, under the instigation of the Romish priests, had caused the massacre, which contained the following passage:—"If all the tyrants of all times and ages were alive again, certainly they would be ashamed when they should find that they had contrived nothing in comparison with these things that might be reputed barbarous and inhuman." The poetical fervour of Milton gave forth the following noble invocation:—

"Avenge, O Lord, Thy slaughtered saints, whose bones
Lie scattered on the Alpine mountains cold!

*   *   *   *   *

Forget not; in Thy book record their groans
Who were Thy sheep, and in their ancient fold,
Slain by the bloody Piedmontese, that rolled
Mother with infant down the rocks. Their moans
The vales redoubled to the hills, and they to heaven."

The result of these circumstances was the delusive treaty of Pinerolo, agreed to in the month of August, 1655. This treaty was hurried on in spite of the request of the plenipotentiaries from England and Holland for a delay, in order that they might secure better terms for the inhabitants of the valleys. While freedom of worship was promised, it was restricted by many irksome conditions; *e.g.*, preaching was forbidden in the commune of S. Giovanni and the town of La Torre, and, moreover, the castle of the latter place was rebuilt and garrisoned, a grievance which the Vaudois had especially protested against. The grievances which grew out of the treaty of Pinerolo, and the events which preceded that ill-conditioned arrangement in the interval between the week of massacre and the date of its signature, are so closely connected with the exploits and history of Janavello, that I feel it better to let my account of La Torre rest here, and proceed to narrate my visit to Rora, the residence of that patriotic soldier and pious chieftain.

CHAPTER IX.

RORA AND JANAVELLO.

In order to reach this spot, my companion and I left the town of La Torre by a street bounded on one side by Trinity College. We then crossed the Pelice by a somewhat rustic bridge, and found ourselves very quickly immersed in woods on the mountain side with numberless bye-paths. These paths were very circuitous, and we had occasion often to ask our way from some friendly woodman or inhabitant of a wayside chalêt. Every now and then we came to a kind of table-land, where we could indulge in a panoramic survey. The steepness of the ascent, and the occasional ruggedness of our path, served to intensify our realization of the interest of the locality, as the scene of so many heroic deeds by Janavello and his little but brave band of patriots against the assailants of their hearths, faith, and homes. About an hour and a half from the time we had left La Torre we came to the Plas Janavel, which constitutes a magnificent amphitheatre, planted with vines, and corn, and chestnut trees. From this locality we bore away in a south-westerly direction, over a rocky eminence crowned with wood, and descended through gardens and orchards to a kind of ravine or narrow valley, on the sloping side of which stands Janavello's house. We found an old, but obliging, Roman Catholic in possession of the premises, once so bravely defended by their patriotic owner. However, overwhelmed by numbers, he was compelled to retreat after performing prodigies of valour, his sister, with babe at her breast, being shot by his side. We were shown the entrance to the subterranean outlet by which Janavello made his escape. The initials G. G., with the date of the year, we also read, cut in the stone above.

So soon, however, as Janavello had placed his little son, only eight years of age, in the care of friends in Dauphiny, he returned to his native valleys, and became the David of his people against the bands of Philistines who were yet in the land. The skill and bravery already displayed by Janavello in so successfully resisting the troops of Pianezza, led the latter at first to attempt to win over the patriot warrior by offering him a pardon for himself and the safe return of his wife and three daughters (who had been captured at Rora) if he would renounce his "heresy," but threatening him if he refused with the severest treatment. To this Janavello nobly replied, "That there were no torments so cruel, nor death so barbarous, which he would not prefer to abjuration; that if the marquis made his wife and daughters to pass through the fire, the flames could only consume their bodies; that as for their souls, he commended them to God, trusting them in His hands equally with his own, in case it should please Him to permit his falling into the hands of the executioners."

Janavello's troop, led by himself and his lieutenant, Jahier, had many successful contests with the enemy during the months of May, June, and July. They captured the town of Secondo, occupied by their enemies, and while putting to death large numbers of the Irish soldiers who had been guilty of such enormities, they yet spared the sick, aged, and children, unlike the treatment accorded to themselves. One of their chief services, however, was to keep in check the garrison which had been placed in the fort at La Torre. A splendid victory on the heights of Angrogna was sadly clouded by a wound received by Janavello. For a time it was thought to be mortal. However, Janavello, being removed to a distance, gradually recovered; but a yet worse thing happened later in the day. Jahier, to whom the command had been entrusted by Janavello, with the request to cease the conflict for that evening, was induced by a traitor to disregard that instruction, and fell, with fifty of his men, into an ambush of the enemy. Jahier, his son, and all his companions but one, fell, covered with wounds, and fighting with the courage of heroes. Leger speaks of Jahier as a perfect captain, had it not have been for his imprudent boldness.

However, Janavello mercifully recovered from his wound, and when the Vaudois, wearied beyond endurance by the cruelties inflicted upon them by the successive governors of that fort at La Torre which had been most unjustly restored in 1655 after its destruction by the French in 1593, could no longer submit, the hero of Rora (notwithstanding a price was set upon his head) assembled some two or three hundred patriots to resist the plundering bands of De Bagnol and Paolo de Berges. Such was the terror caused by these wretches that the people of Giovanni, La Torre, Rora, and Lucerna, fled to the mountains on the French territory. Then, as if disappointed of his prey, De Bagnol issued an edict commanding them within three days to return and present themselves at the fort. No exception was to be allowed for age, sex, or condition. The majority were wise enough to disobey this order, but some, thinking they might be allowed to cultivate their lands again, ventured to return, but, alas! they had occasion to bitterly lament the result. Whilst the commandant of the fortress of La Torre ordered the fugitives to return, Janavello exerted his influence to keep them back. Before the final date, June 25th, 1662, had arrived, an army, commanded by the Marquises of Fleury and Angrogna, appeared at the entrance of the Val Pelice, so that the Vaudois could no longer doubt the intentions of their enemies. But at this stage happened one of those remarkable displays of loyalty to their prince on the part of the Vaudois which was only equalled by their fidelity to God. The troops of the duke were prevented by the armed population of the valleys from crossing the end so as to reach the fort of Mirabouc beyond Bobbio, which was then destitute of provisions, and which it was desired to reinforce. Under these circumstances the commanders of the Piedmontese troops requested the chief persons of the commune to give a proof of submission and good-will to their sovereign by escorting a convoy which was on its way to the fortress. They were assured that if they would do this that peace would be promptly restored. The devoted Vaudois, more willing to risk their own safety than appear to distrust their prince, complied with this request; yea, even more than once, though a war of extermination was being urged against them; for their enemies, unable to discover any marks of merit in those they stigmatized as heretics, were seeking to occupy the heights of La Vachere and obtain possession of their citadel, the Pra del Torre. On the 6th of July, 1663, the enemy ascended the mountains from four different points. The two first divisions, numbering four thousand men, were fortifying themselves on the hill of Plans before attempting to force through the narrow pass called the gate of Angrogna, occupied by a detachment of Vaudois placed there by Janavello. In the meantime the two other divisions of the enemy's force, approaching from the side of Giovanni and La Torre, repulsed the six or seven hundred mountaineers who had been hastily gathered at that point; but when they reached the rocks and ruins of Roccamanetto, the scene of many a victory won by the patriot bands, and which, said Janavello on this occasion, is "our Tabor," the Vaudois stayed the course of their assailants and finally compelled them to retreat with considerable slaughter. Janavello then gave thanks to God, and after leaving a guard led his troops down the valley, exclaiming, "Let us sweep these cowards from the hills!"

After a determined charge in flank, and the renewed efforts of the Vaudois already posted at the gate of Angrogna, the Piedmontese fled, leaving behind them over six hundred dead, besides many wounded. As the results of these discomfitures, a new general was appointed for the Piedmontese troops, Count Damian; and although other successes followed the arms of the patriots, yet they suffered a reverse at St. Germano, and frightful cruelties were perpetrated by their enemies; *e.g.*, at Roccapiatta they burnt to death a woman nearly one hundred years of age, and bedridden. At St. Germano a young woman is treated with every possible indecency, and then left to die, after having her flesh cut from her bones. Other atrocities also were wrought upon persons falling into the hands of the soldiers, which it is impossible to recite. The Duke of Savoy now began to feel disappointed at the results of this persecution of his subjects; and the deputies of the Swiss cantons tried to obtain honourable conditions for the Vaudois. Therefore a kind of amnesty was published Feb. 14th, 1664, which, although professing to confirm the articles of the treaty of Pinerolo, really abridged many of the privileges formerly enjoyed by the Vaudois. It also imposed a fine of two million francs. Janavello was refused any share in the benefits of this treaty, and consequently retired to Geneva, where his valuable counsel stood Arnaud in good stead at a later period. In the war between Charles

Emmanuel of Savoy and the Genoese, in 1672, the Vaudois rendered such cheerful and valuable help that their sovereign was constrained to make a public acknowledgment of their services. A brighter day now seemed dawning upon these faithful valley men. To be the object of their ruler's confidence and affection was a pleasure as sweet to their taste as rare in their experience. But, alas! this pleasant change is but a break in the dark clouds which have so long overshadowed their troubled life, and but the precursor of a storm of bitterness and cruelty unsurpassed even in their annals of woe and sadness. Charles Emmanuel died on the 3rd of June, 1678. For a few years, under the regency of his widow and the reign of his son, Victor Amadeus VII., there was peace. But just at the time when their services against the banditti of Mondovi might seem to have added to their claims and expectation, new dangers appear.

It was in this wise. Louis XIV. of France thought to atone for the misdeeds of a life of sensuality by the forced conversion of his subjects to popery, and so, after a series of preliminary brutalities, to which he had been stimulated by his confessor and others, he revokes the edict of Nantes, and gives to the prosperity of his country a blow from which it has never recovered. But the grand monarque of France was not content to tread this royal road to heaven alone. He wished his neighbour of Savoy to share in the benedictions of the pretended successor of St. Peter. However, the young duke shrank from imitating such conduct, until he was politely reminded by the French ambassador that his master would drive away the heretics with fourteen thousand men, but that he would also retain their valleys for himself. In consequence of this Amadeus engages to join with the king of France in shedding the blood of the saints. A painful foreboding of suffering filled the minds of the Vaudois as soon as they heard of the revocation of the edict of Nantes; but they were not prepared for the actual severity of the edict of January 30th, 1686, which forbade, under pain of death, all religious services except the Romish, and ordered the destruction of their temples, the banishment of their ministers and schoolmasters, and the baptism and education of their children henceforth in the false creed of Rome. This was indeed the bitterest drop in their cup of overflowing grief. Staggered by the enormity of the evil, they first of all sought the ear of their own prince. Disappointed, they began to make preparations to defend themselves against the troops which were gathering on their frontiers. On the 22nd of April the popish army began its march, the Piedmontese led by Gabriel of Savoy, uncle of the duke, the French commanded by Catinat. The latter began operations in the valley of Clusone. They attacked the Vaudois entrenchments at Pramol, but were so obstinately resisted, although they outnumbered the defenders as six to one, that after ten hours' fighting they fell back, followed by the Vaudois as far as the temple of St. Germain, when the night closed the encounter; and on the next day they were protected by reinforcements from Pinerolo. The five hundred Frenchmen killed and wounded on this occasion furnished the pretext for horrible cruelties practised by that portion of the troops which were commanded by Catinat himself in the defenceless valley of Martino.

In the meantime Gabriel of Savoy was attacking the valley of Angrogna. The Vaudois, although weakened by divisions, and lacking such leaders as Janavello and Leger, yet fortified the heights of La Vachere, and for a whole day successfully resisted their assailants. But, unfortunately, they were induced to believe the promise made to them in a note signed by Gabriel of Savoy, in the name of his nephew, that "if they laid down their arms they should not be injured, either in their own persons or in those of their wives and children." This promise, and similar ones made to other groups of the Vaudois at Pra del Torre, Permian, near Pramol, and other retired spots in the neighbourhood of La Torre, were all shamefully disregarded. The people of Bobbio were the last to give way, after a brave resistance, which they continued on the rocks of the Vandalin. Frightful deeds of shame and cruelty now prevailed all through the valleys. Two examples may suffice, although by no means the worst in some respects. A woman takes refuge in a cave, with her little babe and a goat, which furnished the means of their subsistence. Unfortunately the poor animal was heard to bleat by some of the soldiers who happened to be near. These wretches seized the child and, in the presence of its mother, threw it over the precipice, and then led the mother herself to a jutting crag that she might die there in the greatest agony. A second case is that of the pastor of Guigot, near Prali. He had secreted himself under a rock, and believing the enemy to be at a distance, was consoling himself by singing a psalm. For this offence, after months of suffering in prison, he was condemned to death. He died with the Saviour's words on his lips—"Father, into thy hands I commend my spirit." The cruelties inflicted on the Vaudois at this time were even greater than those resulting from the massacres of 1655; but, in addition to all that took place within the valleys themselves, there remain the wrongs perpetrated upon those who were dragged from their loved, though desolated, homes. Some fourteen thousand persons were distributed in thirteen or fourteen prison fortresses. Husbands were separated from their wives, parents from their children, some two thousand children being placed among papists for the purposes of perversion. These were chiefly sent to the district of Vercelli, in Piedmont. And thus the church of Rome won a triumph even more complete than her sanguinary labours in the low countries. She had now silenced the gospel in Italy. That pure flame in the valleys of Piedmont no longer shone amidst the darkness. Those pious mountaineers no longer sang their psalms by hill-side, nor offered the worship of a free heart in their lowly dells. The pure morals of those shepherds and vine-dressers no longer rebuked the foul licentiousness which flourished amid the benedictions of

Santa Chiesa, provided heretics were exterminated. That gospel which apostles taught, and Rome once received, was no longer heard from the lips of pastors who disdain the polluting touch of hands more able to confer the gifts of Simon Magus than those of Simon Peter.

But yet these children of a pure faith are not conquered. They leave their homes in the months of November, December, and February. Hundreds perish by the way. How could it be otherwise? At that season of the year, and after the treatment they had received in the dungeons in which they had groaned, even strong men would have shrank from crossing the Alps, to say nothing of the aged women and young children. Alas! O Rome, thy tender mercies are cruel! The Swiss Protestants did nobly to soften the horrors of the treatment awarded to their suffering co-religionists. They not only remonstrated at the Court of Turin, but provided clothing and food to assist the sufferers; they kept a solemn fast-day; they made collections; they stationed themselves, by the consent of the Piedmontese authorities (let it be said), at various places along the route. So by the end of February, 1687, some two thousand six hundred Vaudois, men, women, and children, were received within the hospitable walls of the city of Geneva. Afterwards their numbers reached three thousand, and these were all that remained out of a population of about sixteen thousand, dragged or driven from the valleys. Nine pastors had been imprisoned in the citadel of Turin with their families, and although their liberation was earnestly asked for by the Swiss commissioners, it does not appear that they were ever allowed to join their exiled brethren in Switzerland. However, the Vaudois, though deeply touched with the kindness shown them by their friends in Switzerland and Germany, yet sighed after their own dear valleys. Although Janavello could not lend them active aid by his no longer stalwart arm and heroic presence, yet he took a deep interest in the preparations for their return, and praised God that He had provided them a captain. Who this captain was, and the nature of the deliverance wrought by his instrumentality, must be left for another chapter.

CHAPTER X.

Henri Arnaud was born at Die, in Dauphiny, in 1641. He was educated for the Christian ministry, but, owing to the troubles of the period, betook himself to a military life for a time. He entered the service of William Prince of Orange, afterwards King William III. of England, who was regarded at that time as the hereditary champion of Protestant interests in Europe, and the determined opponent, as he afterwards proved, of the restless ambition and persecuting tyranny of Louis XIV. of France. The Prince of Orange thought highly of the military talents and the personal character of Henri Arnaud, and promoted him to the rank of captain in his army. He seems, however, to have reverted to the intention of his early life, about the year 1684, inasmuch as we find him occupying the important post of pastor at La Torre during the eventful year 1686, the year of the revocation of the edict of Nantes. Amadeus II., goaded on by the threatenings and entreaties of the French king, renewed the persecution of his faithful Vaudois, by the publication of a severe edict in January, and by the invasion of their territory in the April following. The Vaudois defended themselves with such courage and success that, after ten hours' fighting, the invaders were compelled to retreat as far as the temple at Germano. The close of the day gave a respite to the enemy, and enabled them to obtain reinforcements from Pinerolo. In this successful repulse of the French and Piedmontese troops, and which resulted in the death or wounding of 500 Frenchmen, Henri Arnaud played a conspicuous part. But when subsequently the Vaudois were ready to confide in the faithless but plausible proposals of Gabriel of Savoy, Henri Arnaud refused to trust himself to the enemies of his country, and as his warnings were disregarded he escaped to Switzerland. Here he was providentially preserved and protected for a yet greater opportunity of service to the land and church of his adoption. The promise of Gabriel of Savoy to the Vaudois, that if they laid down their arms they should not be injured, either in their own persons or in those of their wives and children, was shamefully disregarded; therefore, after terrible sufferings in the summer and autumn, several thousands quit their much-loved valleys, and cross the Alps in the worst season of the year rather than abjure the faith of their fathers. About two thousand six hundred of these exiles reach the hospitable city of Geneva by the end of February, 1687. Later on some hundreds more were added to their numbers. Beside Henry Arnaud, there was already at Geneva the heroic Janavello. Deeply touched as were the exiles with the Christian sympathy shown to them by friends in Switzerland and Germany, gratefully impressed as they were with the efforts making for their settlement in these hospitable countries, yet their thoughts would often revert to their native valleys. They not only sighed over the remembrance of the pastures where they had fed their flocks, but they also groaned for the temples of

God which had been broken down. For the voice of truth which was now silenced in the land of martyrs and confessors, and simultaneously grew up the hope and the desire of returning to the place which had been for so long the home of their fathers. When Henri Arnaud found that this project had the approval of the veteran Janavello, he repaired to Holland, to lay the design before the Prince of Orange, who warmly entered into the design, and promised substantial assistance towards its realization. After two premature attempts and many difficulties, Arnaud, who was residing at this time with his family at Neufchâtel, made his arrangements so well that many hundreds of the Vaudois succeeded in assembling in the forest of Prangins, near the little town of Nyon on the shore of the lake Leman.

Between nine and ten o'clock in the evening of the 16th of August, 1689, Arnaud gave the signal for embarkation by falling on his knees by the side of the lake, and imploring in a loud voice the almighty and all-gracious Being, who had been their helper in the past, to prosper their attempt to regain their native valleys, and re-erect the standard of evangelical truth on their own beloved fatherland. The patriot band set out in fifteen boats, and having landed, the first detachment returned for those left behind. Only three of the boats, however, made the second journey in safety, and so some were not brought from the Swiss side of the lake. When Arnaud reviewed his forces he found there were some 900 men who had safely crossed the lake. A small band indeed for so great an enterprise; a very inadequate force to contend with thousands of disciplined troops, and to overcome the obstacles which would be raised by hostile populations through whose territories they must pass; to encounter the fatigue of forced marches over craggy precipices, along deep and dangerous defiles—in addition, to do all this with but slender equipments of food and other necessaries. Still, no one draws back. They have counted the cost. They deem the prize at which they aim worthy of the risk they run. They are sustained by the recollections of past deliverance. "Our fathers trusted in Thee, and Thou didst deliver them; they cried unto Thee, and were delivered; they trusted in Thee, and were not confounded," was the sentiment which sped them onward in their arduous march. Nor did Arnaud neglect any suitable means of an ordinary kind for ensuring success. He divided his 900 men into twenty companies, organized with reference to their native communes; *e.g.*, Angrogna had three companies, with their captains; San Giovanni two, &c. They were arranged to march in regular military order, having a vanguard, centre, and rear, observing the strictest discipline. Beside Arnaud, there were two other pastors with the little army, Chyon of Pont à Royans, in Dauphiny, and Montoux of the Val Pragela. The first, however, was soon lost to the expedition; for, having incautiously entered the first village they reached in order to obtain a guide, he was taken prisoner, and detained at Chambéry until the peace. As soon as the army was ready to march, the patriot band again sought the blessing of the God of their fathers. They then set out in a southerly direction, passing through the little town of Yvoire, and compelled Savoyard gentlemen and priests to accompany them as hostages and guides. The alarm felt at first by the people through whose villages they passed subsided when their orderly conduct became known, so that after a time the peasants, with their ministers, were seen approaching and watching the troops as they filed off, and even crying after them, "May God be with you!" In some cases refreshments were also supplied, and remuneration refused. However, a different experience awaited them as they set out by a mountain path for Boëge, a little town on the river Menoge, in the province of Faucigny. Here the gentry made a great show of resistance, and although they made them prisoners, together with 200 armed peasants under the command of a quartermaster, yet the circumstance convinced Arnaud that he must take precautions, otherwise the expedition would be greatly hindered. Therefore one of the gentry of Boëge was instructed to write a letter informing the people of the next town that they were not to be alarmed at the approach of the Vaudois, but to give them a free passage, and supply them with provisions, for which they always paid. So they passed on without very remarkable events, except privations and exposure to wet and cold day by day, until, crossing the Arve, they reached Sallenches, at the foot of the mighty monarch of European mountains, Mont Blanc. The sight of the mountain seems to have severely tested the resolution of some of Arnaud's followers, and it required all his skill and energy to inspire them with courage to make the passage through the defile of the Bonhomme. Indeed, the descent of the column was more hazardous than the ascent. To accomplish this in many cases they were compelled to assume a sitting posture, and slide down the face of the rocks. On the evening of the fourth day the patriots reached the town of Sey, on the Isère, and met with a good supply of provisions. On the evening of the fifth day Arnaud and his colleague, Montoux, for the first time since they had started, lodged, supped, and rested for three hours in peace. The next day they ascended Mont Iseran, and resting at Maurienne in the evening, they ascended the Mont Cenis the day after, and seized all the post-horses, to prevent the news of their arrival being so easily communicated. From this point they branched off in the direction of the little Mont Cenis, as being a less frequented road, and spent the night very uncomfortably in the woods.

On the eighth day they left the valley of Jaillon, and would have proceeded by way of Susa, crossing the Dora Riparia, but having unsuccessfully attempted to dislodge a body of troops and peasants who commanded a portion of that road, Arnaud decided on regaining the heights. This they did, but not without much suffering and a loss of forty men, including two captains and two surgeons. After this the Vaudois proceeded through the pass of Touille, to the west, coming out by Oulx, still in the valley of the Dora, but several leagues distant from Susa, and in the line now traversed by the masterpiece of modern engineering, viz., the Mont Cenis Tunnel. Arnaud's design was to cross the river by the bridge of Salabertrand, between Oulx and Exilles, but learning from a peasant, of whom they had asked for food, that an excellent supper was preparing for them, they understood it was dangerous to remain. After taking refreshment, therefore, Arnaud renewed the march, and discovered some thirty-six camp fires, and shortly after the vanguard encountered the enemy's outposts.

As was the invariable custom, an interval of prayer preceded their further advance, made under cover of the night. Approaching the bridge, they are asked, "Who's there?" and answer, "Friends;" to which the enemy reply, "Kill! kill!" emphasized by a tremendous fire for a quarter of an hour. Arnaud, however, saved his men by commanding them to lie on the ground at the first shot. Still they were in great danger, for a portion of the enemy had got to the rear of the Vaudois, and so they were exposed from both sides. Realizing their desperate position, a cry was raised—"Courage! the bridge is won!" At those words Arnaud's men rushed headlong, sword in hand, and with bayonets fixed forced the entrenchments of the enemy. Thus, by the favour of God, 800 men, unaccustomed to war, and exhausted by fatigue, won a victory over a body numbering some 2,500 troops, exclusive of those who had attacked them in the rear, and the peasants who assisted in the fray. The defeated lost six hundred of their men, besides twelve captains and other officers; the victors, only fifteen killed and twelve wounded. Their hostages, however, took advantage of the battle and escaped, with the exception of six of the oldest. Apart from the successful repulse of the troops intended to obstruct their journey, this splendid victory at the bridge of Salabertrand gave to the conquerors military stores and other booty. Arnaud's men would have been glad to have rested, but prudence bid them not to linger. So, having destroyed so much of the spoil as they were unable to appropriate, they set forward. The explosion of the enemy's powder, set on fire by the Vaudois, mingled with their own shouts of triumph and the notes of their trumpets, as with exulting hearts they renewed their march, exclaiming, "Thanks be to the Lord of hosts, who hath given us the victory over all our enemies." However great as was their joy, so great had been their labours that twenty-four of their number were so overpowered by fatigue that they fell asleep on their moonlight march through the valley of the Dora, and were captured by the enemy, so that these twenty-four added to the forty previously lost in the passage of the Jaillon, diminished the full measure of their satisfaction. Still they press forward, and as the light of another day dawns upon them (the ninth of their journey and the Lord's Day) they had climbed the summit of Mont Sci, and from it looked with beating hearts upon the peaks of their own loved mountains. Indeed it was only the valley of Pragela (a district closely associated with their own in faith and worship until his so-called Christian majesty banished the profession of the gospel from its boundaries) that interposed between them and the object of their march. On this Pisgah top Arnaud gathers his men around him, and beneath the roof of heaven and amidst the walls of surrounding mountain slopes, glistening with the brightness of the rising sun, pours out the psalm of glad thanksgiving, and offers the prayer of the contrite heart.

On Tuesday, August 27th, 1689, the brave Vaudois, who had crossed the lake of Geneva only eleven days before, now set foot in the first village of their own territory, viz., Balsille, at the north-west extremity of the valley of San Martino. This was indeed a solemn moment, recalling the successful labours of the past and suggesting the difficulties and anxieties of the future. Arnaud would doubtless examine minutely into the condition and number of his men, and as he did so painfully consider the losses he had sustained, reducing the patriot band to about seven hundred men. This review is necessary in order to explain the otherwise sanguinary character of the determination to refuse all quarter to the troops which attacked them in their endeavours to regain possession of their native valleys. Hence the Vaudois put to death the guard on the Alps of the Pis, and at Balsille; this was the greatest number they did so treat. From Balsille Arnaud led his men into the valley of Prali, and subdivided his army into two divisions. On reaching the hamlet of Guigot, they rejoiced to find their temple still standing, and purging it of the superstitious ornaments introduced by the Papists, these seven hundred patriot warriors laid down their arms and sang the 74th Psalm—

"Hast Thou cast us off for ever?
Will Thine anger no more cease?
Shall Thy people never, never
Dwell again, O Lord, in peace?
Oh, behold the desolation!
See Thy holy place defiled!
Scattered is Thy congregation,
And Thy sanctuary spoiled.

"Rise, O Lord, in might victorious,
Rise and give Thy people aid;
Come, O come in triumph glorious,
Overwhelm Thy foes dismayed.
Circled with a thousand wonders,
Girt with all Thy power and strength,
Mid ten thousand thousand thunders
Save, redeem Thy own, at length!"

They also sung the 129th Psalm, and then Arnaud, taking his text from some verses of the latter psalm, spoke to them, and exhorted them to endure hardness as good soldiers of Jesus Christ. The memories of the place as the scene of the martyrdom of the pastor Leydet, who was barbarously put to death near this spot by Papists who overheard him singing psalms, would tend to deepen their emotion and fill their souls with firmer resolves to dare and die for faith and fatherland.

Their courage soon found employment in dislodging a body of 200 troops who were entrenched at the ports of San Guliano. These men contemptuously dared them to the fight, shouting, "Come on, varlets of the devil, we occupy all the passes, and there are three thousand of us!" The Vaudois accepted the challenge, and at a single charge drove them from their trenches and captured all their stores, a very valuable acquisition to the conquerors. Moreover they slew thirty-one of the fugitives, and lost but one of their own number. Following up their successes, they besieged Bobbio, and drove away those who had dispersed its rightful and former occupants. After this they hold a solemn conclave for devotional and deliberative purposes. M. Montoux, Arnaud's colleague in the pastoral office, addressed them, and then Arnaud himself read the following oath, which was solemnly agreed to, viz., "God, by His divine grace, having happily reconducted us to the inheritance of our fathers, there to establish the pure service of our holy religion, ... we, pastors, captains, and other officers, swear and promise before the face of the living God, ... neither to separate nor disunite while God grants us life, even should we have the misfortune to be reduced to three or four.... And to the intent that union, which is the soul of our affairs, should remain inviolable among us, the officers shall swear fidelity to the soldiers, and the soldiers to the officers, promising together to our Lord and Saviour Jesus Christ to deliver, if possible, our brethren from the cruel woman of Babylon, and with them to re-establish and maintain his kingdom till death, and observe all our lives with good faith this present ordinance." As I stood upon this consecrated platform (Sibaud), April 11th, 1871, I not only felt richly rewarded for the steep climb, from which the good pastor of Bobbio sought to dissuade me, but I gained an enlarged view of the wonderful power of the gospel of Christ in ennobling and constraining the souls of these valley men to such deeds of daring and suffering. If, as I firmly believe, the gospel teaches that willingness to do and suffer for Christ is the evidence of our belonging to Him, how luminous and abundant are the title-deeds of the Vaudois to be reckoned "not least among the churches of God." May the spirit of the oath still survive, and the day come when every one of those who inhabit the locality shall be as true to the gospel of the grace of God as Arnaud and his brave troops!

After this solemn convocation, and sundry additions to their military organization, an attempt was made by Arnaud to rescue Villaro from the Papists as Bobbio was rescued. At the first the enemy fled, some across the Pelice, and others to the convent. While the Vaudois were closely pressing them in this last-named retreat, their own position was turned by the arrival of a large body of troops. These troops, 12,000 in number, drove back the Vaudois to Bobbio, and threatened to exterminate them all. Eighty made good their escape over the Vandalin by scattering themselves in all directions, and afterwards rejoining the main body. Montoux, the assistant pastor, being thus separated from his friends, was captured by the enemy, and detained a prisoner at Turin until the peace. Arnaud three times gave himself up for lost. Three times, with six of his men, he betook himself to prayer; and three times the Lord sent him deliverance. At last he escaped to the same mountain ridge where the eighty previously dispersed awaited his arrival.

The check received at Villaro led Arnaud to retire from the inhabited parts of the valley of Lucerna to the mountain heights, from which they could attack detachments of troops at favourable intervals, and to which they could betake themselves for safety in spots difficult of access, and easily defended by a small number against large bodies of troops. These mountain recesses, indeed, play an important part in the history of the Vaudois generally, as well as in the exploits of Janavello and Arnaud in particular. One of our sweetest English poets has beautifully apostrophized the feelings of the brave valley men in the following exquisite lines:—

"For the strength of the hills we bless Thee,
Our God, our fathers' God!
Thou hast made Thy children mighty
By the touch of the mountain sod,
Thou hast fixed our ark of refuge
Where the spoiler's foot ne'er trod;
For the strength of the hills we bless Thee,
Our God, our fathers' God.

"The banner of the chieftain
Far, far below us waves,
The war-horse of the spearman
Cannot reach our lofty caves.
Thy dark clouds wrap the threshold
Of freedom's last abode;
For the strength of the hills we thank Thee,
Our God, our fathers' God.

"For the shadow of Thy presence,
Round our camp of rock outspread;
For the stern defiles of battle,
Bearing record of our dead;
For the snows and for the torrents,
For the free heart's burial sod;
For the strength of the hills we bless Thee,
Our God, our fathers' God."

It was chiefly on the heights above Sibaud, the slopes of the Vandalin, La Vachera, and Mont Cervin, that they carried on their predatory and guerrilla warfare. At one time they attacked 600 men, killed one hundred, and lost only four. But they suffered almost incredible privations. Their food oftentimes consisting of only wild fruits, raw cabbages, and other vegetables uncooked. Occasionally they met with better fare; *e.g.*, being at Prali for two days they cut down all the corn in the neighbourhood, and ground it at the mills in the place. Nor did they forget their duties as Christians in the midst of all these hardships. Arnaud administered the holy communion to the troops who were with him, as well as to those in retreat above Bobbio. The retreat of the Piedmontese troops under the command of the Marquis de Parelle, enabled the Vaudois to keep in possession of the valley of San Martino, and to lay up a stock of corn, grapes, chestnuts, apples, and walnuts. The flying camp also were able to capture some convoys of provision, so that they could look forward to the winter (this was now Sept. 16th) without much fear as to supplies. The Vaudois were now in three divisions; the larger part in the valley of San Martino, another body next in number who were scouring the valley of Angrogna, and the third and smaller division at Serre de Cruel over Bobbio. This last detachment destroyed the convent of Villaro lest it should be turned into a fortress. They pulled down the popish church at Rora, reduced the village to ashes, and brought away much spoil. However, as soon as the Piedmontese soldiers were able to cover the mountains with troops they retaliated by setting on fire the Vaudois asylum at Serre de Cruel. The Vaudois resisted, and did much execution; but at last, terrified by the numbers of their adversaries, they forsook their new fortifications at Pausettes and Aiguille, leaving behind them all their winter stores. They were pursued from rock to rock, obliged to hide in the most loathsome caverns, and to subsist almost without food, which was procured only at the peril of their lives. Nothing but a special Providence kept them from entire destruction, and enabled them to rejoin the main body of their friends in the valley of San Martino. The French troops engaged in thus hunting the Vaudois in the month of October were commanded by M. de l'Ombraille, and, with the Piedmontese under Parelle, covered all the villages and passes excepting a few small hamlets and byways. Hence the position of the patriots was one of great danger. Some deserted, and perished miserably by the enemy. A council was held at Rodoret. Divisions of opinion arose, and ruin seemed at hand. At this critical moment Arnaud summoned them to prayer. After this he exhorted his companions to sacrifice their own views for the common good, and advised a retreat upon Balsille. This they happily consented to, and the same night they were on their way to the spot. The dangers of the road may be supposed from the circumstance that much of it had to be passed on their hands and knees, and from the fact that when the Vaudois afterwards saw the places by daylight they were filled with horror.

We shall not be able to realize the good Providence which befriended them at this time unless we consider for a moment the exact position of their new retreat. The chief group of houses in the village of Balsille is close to a torrent at the foot of the mountains in the extreme north-west of the Val Martino. A stone bridge, close to which is a mill, unites the two parts of the village lying eastward, at the foot of the steep rocks of Guignivert, which rises towards the west, and is thickly wooded at its base.[E]

From this natural wall a rock projects against the river and over the dwellings, forming quite a natural fortress. It was supplied with water by three fountains. On this rock, then, the Vaudois determined to await the enemy, instead of fleeing from mountain to mountain as they had previously done. To this end they excavated, threw up entrenchments, made covered ways, and executed a series of defences in harmony with what might have been the suggestions of a skilful military engineer. They had three lines of defence within the fortifications on the lower rock, and then, on an eminence yet higher, they constructed a little fort, with triple entrenchment, and lastly, overlooking all, they posted a watch to give notice of the least movement of the enemy. In addition to this they repaired the mill at the foot of their fortifications. During this Arnaud preached twice a week and conducted daily prayer. The Vaudois had only been a few days at their work, when the French battalions, unable to meet with them at Rodoret, followed them down the valley, having already surprised their outposts at Passet, though without inflicting loss. On the 29th of October the enemy surrounded them with troops from Friday to Sunday. They also tried to force the bridge, but were compelled to retreat, leaving sixty men killed and as many wounded, while the Vaudois had not lost a man. In the month of November the French captured one of Arnaud's men, who had gone to nurse a sick friend, and in spite of the entreaties of the judge at Pérousé, a Roman Catholic, the commandant, De l'Ombraille, insisted on his execution. They made no further assault upon the castle, but having burnt all the houses, farm buildings, corn stacks, &c., they retired, telling the Vaudois "to have patience, and they would return after Easter." They were now comparatively free in their movements, and felt intensely thankful to that gracious Father who had preserved them through so many dangers, and given them, to retain possession of, the land they had come to reclaim. They were about 400 strong, exclusive of that division which had fixed itself on the mountains of Angrogna, and the two little bands which still found a refuge in the wilds of the glen Guichard, or among the rocks overhanging Bobbio.

The question of food made them anxious. But that God who had so wonderfully provided for them in the past, had made as remarkable provision for this necessity. A fall of snow had covered the corn which had ripened in September, but was left standing in the fields by this circumstance. Thus hidden from the enemy, a sudden thaw revealed the treasure thus mercifully laid up for these patriot warriors. In addition to the corn, strong detachments made requisitions on the valleys of Pragela and Queyras, and so obtained supplies of butter, salt, wine, and other provisions. A sad incident of the winter arose from the condition of one of those little parties, whom the chances of war or some imprudence separated from the main body. A band of twelve, concealed in a cave behind L'Essart, near Bobbio, were obliged by hunger to come out for provisions. On returning, they thought they had been tracked in the snow, and so decided to betake themselves to a new place of refuge in La Biava. Scarcely had they set out, however, than they discovered 125 peasants in pursuit of them. They threw down their baggage, and having reached a commanding height, poured down such an effective volley that their assailants sought a truce, and acknowledged twelve dead and thirteen wounded, though not one of the Vaudois was the least hurt. Their victory did not, however, relieve them for long. Although their refuge was secure, the extreme cold made it untenable, and they were compelled to seek a milder climate. Saddened by suffering, and resolved to protect themselves, they met on their way an armed band. Assuming that they were enemies, they fired and killed one of the party, when, to their great grief, blended with unutterable joy, they discovered that they were brethren. With tears in their eyes they embraced each other, and found the safety and succour they had almost despaired of in the castle at Balsille.

During the winter months messages were sent to induce the Vaudois to withdraw from their native land. To this Arnaud sent suitable replies, and also strengthened the fortifications in the only part which had been left open by the river side.

On the 1st of May, 12,000 Piedmontese troops and 10,000 French, making a total of 22,000 troops, under the command of Catinat, surrounded Arnaud's retreat. A body of horse soldiers concealed themselves in the neighbouring woods, but were received with so effective a discharge of shot as to inflict great loss. The main body of the assailants drew up to the foot of the rock, but had to make a rapid retreat, with severe loss both in dead and wounded. After this an engineer, having surveyed the approaches to the castle through a glass, ordered a picked corps of 500 men to advance in that direction, supported by some 700 peasants of Pragela and Queyras, for the purpose of destroying the fence of trees and palisades constructed by Arnaud. Their attack was covered by the fire of 700 men, drawn up in line of battle. But all was in vain; the fortifications were impregnable, and the Vaudois, taking advantage of their confusion, poured down upon them with such vigour that only ten or twelve men escaped. The commander and two sergeants who remained by his side were taken prisoners, but not a single Vaudois was injured. The enemy retreated in great confusion, and Arnaud, assembling his men for thanksgiving and prayer, spoke so powerfully that both pastor and people, officers and men, were affected to tears. On searching the bodies of the slain, a number of popish charms were found, vainly used as preservatives against the attacks of men who were supposed to be in league with the evil one.

Catinat, like the Marquis de Larcy, in the affair of the bridge at Salabertrand, was so mortified at his want of success, that he declined to head another assault against the Vaudois, therefore he entrusts the command to the Marquis de Fequières. This new attack, on the 10th of May, deprived Arnaud and his men of the privilege of the Holy Communion, which they had desired to partake of on Whit Monday. The day following that on which the enemy's vanguard was observed, de Fequières formed his men into five divisions, and completely invested the Vaudois stronghold. Finding the discharge of musketry useless, he planted a cannon, loaded with balls weighing eight pounds, on the Mont Guignivert, exactly opposite to La Balsille. He then hoisted a white flag, and afterwards a red, signifying that unless the besieged asked for peace that no quarter would be granted. They had previously refused to surrender, on the ground "that they looked to the aid of God to protect them in the heritage of their fathers, but that if it were otherwise, they would not yield while life lasted."

The day following a breach was made, and an assault directed to three different points. The attacking columns were covered by a furious cannonade, and yet, wonderful to relate, none of the defenders were struck. However, the lower entrenchments had to be abandoned, and M. de Parat, the French prisoner, put to death, he acknowledging the necessity of the sentence. Indeed, a crisis had come. Balsille could not be defended much longer. The watch on the summit had been driven away by the enemy commanding the opposite rocks. Happily the darkness was coming on, and by its aid one means of safety was looked for, viz., flight. But when the Vaudois looked out upon the glare of the enemy's camp fires their hearts almost sank within them. And the French, on their part, were joyfully anticipating their speedy destruction. But He who had so often fought for

Israel only permitted them to be reduced to such straits that they might learn afresh how completely He was on their side. The camp fires, having by their light revealed a possibility of escape through a frightful ravine, were extinguished, so far as service to the enemy was concerned, *by means of a thick fog*! So under cover of this shield of the Almighty the devoted band, led by Captain Poulat, a native of Balsille, let themselves down by an opening in the rocks. The journey was one of great difficulty. Branches of trees and projecting ledges of rocks were used to assist the descent, which was chiefly made in a sitting or sliding posture. Nor could the fugitives altogether escape the neighbourhood of the French patrols, so closely were they posted to the castle. One of the Vaudois, using his hands to save himself from falling, let drop a kettle he was carrying, which by its rolling down excited the notice of the sentinel, who at once gave the challenge, "Who goes there?" But as the kettle made no reply, the men passed on, Arnaud humorously relates. After descending the precipitous sides of Mont Guignivert, the Vaudois directed their steps southward towards Salse. It was now two hours after the break of day, and they were cutting steps for themselves in the snow. A portion of the enemy's watch discovered that they had escaped, and gave the alarm. Very quickly the enemy pursued them in their journey, first of all for rest at Salse, then on to Rodoret. Finding this, the Vaudois betook themselves to the summit of Galmon, where they halted, and Arnaud reviewed his men. The sick and wounded were sent to a declivity to be tended by the surgeon of M. Parat, under a strong guard. The main body passed the night in the wood of Serrelémi. A fog fortunately rising, enabled them to advance to a hamlet called La Majère, where a shower of rain gave them a much-needed supply of water. On the 17th of May, 1690 they had a sharp skirmish in the village and churchyard of Pramol. They killed fifty-seven, and captured the commandant, from whom Arnaud learnt that in three days Victor Amadeus would have to decide as to the question of continuing his alliance with France, or of uniting with England and other European states against Louis XIV. Arnaud, who by his former intimacy with the Prince of Orange, now William III. of England, was well acquainted with European politics, at once saw how important was this news, and awaited the result with corresponding anxiety.

The day after (Sunday), whilst Arnaud and his men were on the heights of Angrogna, two messengers, sent by General Palavicini, announced the decision of Victor Amadeus, and offered terms of peace in his name. The sudden pleasure of such a communication, after nine months of hardship, toil, and fighting, might have been too much for these poor persecuted ones, had it not been tempered with doubts as to its truthfulness. But gradually events confirmed their hopes, and scattered their fears. Provisions were sent to Arnaud's men. The ministers, Montoux and Bastie, with others who had been confined at Turin, now hastened to meet their brethren. Everywhere they seemed treated with confidence; and, in conjunction with the Duke's troops, they made several successful attacks upon the French.

One of Arnaud's men having captured a courier carrying despatches for the King of France, Palavicini, commander-in-chief of the troops of Piedmont, was ordered to bring Arnaud with him into the presence of Amadeus. The latter received the Vaudois deputation most graciously, and expressed his desire that they should be henceforth friends, assuring them "that if they hazarded their lives in his service, he also would hazard his for them." In proof of this cordial reconciliation, Amadeus conferred the rank of colonel on the brave Arnaud, the chieftain of the Vaudois. He also granted permission for the families of the banished ones to return to their valleys, and decreed the restoration of their ancient possessions. Early in July Arnaud hastened to Milan to meet the refugees from Switzerland and Germany, who with wives and children set out for their native valleys, aided even by the kind help of those who, like the Elector of Brandenburg, had given them shelter at some expense in his dominions, but who now made fresh sacrifices to gratify the longing of their hearts.

Victor Amadeus was faithful to his promise, and not only allowed the exiles to return to home and faith, but he also consented that some who under the severity of trial had abjured their faith should be allowed the privilege of returning to their first and purer creed. In return for this kindness, as well as in strict conformity with their own patriotic and pious principles, the Vaudois greatly assisted the Duke of Savoy in his war with France, is the testimony of Botta in his *Storia d'Italia*. The Count of Saluzzo also testifies "that they hastened to join the Marquis de Perelle, *who had not long before attacked them*, and that their skirmishes cost the enemy, whom they drove from Lucerna, more than a thousand men." Beauregard, in his "*Historical Memories of the House of Savoy*," says, that "*the barbets*, by their bravery, made themselves formidable to the French;" and with regard to the siege of Coni, mentions with special praise the services of a troop of "eight hundred Vaudois, under the command of a chief celebrated among them." This chief, no doubt, was Arnaud; but whilst he was anxious that they should render to their prince every possible help in a military point of view, the latter sought to carry out his intention of restoring the Vaudois to their property; but there were great difficulties in the way.

By the edict of May 23rd, 1694, the ancient rights of the Vaudois are acknowledged, and the persecuting decrees of January and April, 1686, revoked. The pope, Innocent XII., tried to invalidate the decree, but the Senate of Turin confirmed the edict of their sovereign, and prohibited the bull of the pope.

So, all the prospect seemed fair, and the Vaudois, so long and cruelly persecuted, might hope for an era of prosperity; for the time and means not only to cultivate their desolated vineyards, to lead their flocks again to pasture on their mountain slopes, and rebuild their thatched homesteads, but also to restore the pure worship of their own and their fathers' God. But, alas! "put not your trust in princes" was a sentiment which might have been graven deeply on the memory of the all-confiding, all-enduring Vaudois.

Victor Amadeus was persuaded by the crafty Louis XIV. to forsake his allies in the war against France, and become again a vassal of the proud and perfidious French king. And therefore, while he remains true to the engagement to protect the ancient inhabitants of the valleys against their inveterate persecutor, he makes a secret treaty (1696) by which, firstly, intercourse between the professors of the reformed faith in France and Savoy is prohibited; secondly, French soldiers enlisted in the Vaudois army are no longer allowed to remain in the service of the duke; thirdly, refugees from France were to be expelled the valleys.

This crafty device of the mean and cowardly French king resulted in the banishment of seven of the most valuable Vaudois pastors, viz., Montoux, the companion of Arnaud, five of their colleagues, natives of Pragela or Dauphine, and *Arnaud himself*! It was indeed with a heavy heart that the brave and trusted leader, the tried and sagacious counsellor, the devoted and accomplished pastor of the Vaudois, left for ever those churches in whose service he had wrought such exploits, and on whose behalf he had dared death in a thousand shapes and suffered almost incredible privations. His only consolation, and without it, hero as he was, Arnaud might have died from grief, lay in the mighty fact, that he had been privileged to accomplish a work inferior to none in the annals of history. With a motive infinitely higher than that of Zenophon, his exploits as a soldier are equal in skill, endurance, and bravery to his; while, as regards results, the contrast is still more favourable to Henri Arnaud's work.

The Greeks, it is true, were brought back to their country, but remained mercenaries to the last, while the Vaudois both regained their homes, and succeeded in replanting the standard of their faith so firmly under the favour of Almighty God that never since has it been in such danger of extinction as Arnaud delivered it from.

"Since then 'abide the chosen race
Within their ancient dwelling place,
'Since then 'upon each Alpine height
Truth sits enthroned in Rome's despite.'"

Some 3,000 French Protestants withdrew with Henri Arnaud from the valleys. Their first resting-place was Geneva, which twelve years before had so charitably welcomed the persecuted Vaudois. Arnaud reached Geneva August 30th, 1698, and speedily sought a place of habitation for his brethren. The Duke of Wurtemberg provided a home for these victims of the cruelty of Louis XIV. in a place to the west and north of Stuttgardt. On this occasion the exiles had no hope of returning, and they settled down in their new abode and called their rising settlements by the names of their former villages in the valleys of Perosa and Pragela. The Duke of Wurtemberg treated these people with every kindness. As regards church matters and education they carried out their own home arrangements, assisted by funds from England. In a colony, Schoenberg, near Dürrmenz, Arnaud passed the remainder of his life. He declined the pressing offer of our King William III. to take the command of a regiment in the English army. Having led the Vaudois once back to their native soil, and established them in their earthly Goshen, his only desire now was to lead the flock entrusted to his care amid the green pastures of the gospel upward to the heavenly Canaan.

He died on the 8th of September, 1721, having reached the goodly age of four score years. He was twice married, and left behind him three sons and two daughters.

Within the humble precincts of a temple built with walls of clay, and a bell, whose sound was never heard beyond the cherry-trees of the village, gratitude and respect have assigned a place of honour to the mortal remains of this truly great man. The ashes of Henri Arnaud lie beneath the communion table. An engraving suspended below the pulpit gives the features of the hero of San Germano of Salabertrand and the Balsille.

While on his tombstone is the following Latin inscription:—

"Beneath this Tomb lies

HENRI ARNAUD,

PASTOR AND ALSO MILITARY COMMANDER OF THE PIEDMONTESE VAUDOIS."

In the centre of the monument—

"Thou seest here the ashes of Arnaud, but his achievements, labours, and undaunted courage none can depict. The son of Jesse combats alone thousands of foreigners; alone he terrifies their camp and leader. He died September 8th, 1721, aged lxxx."

FOOTNOTES:

[E] A modern traveller thus graphically describes the place as he saw it in 1854:—"And now came in view the glorious Balsille, springing from the bed of the Germanasca, and its successive wooded aiguilles rising like pinnacles up the steep roof of a Gothic cathedral.... Around it gape fearful ravines, each with its headlong torrent, separating it from the grand heights of the d'Albergian on the north, and the mount Guignivert on the south; whilst it is attached to the summit of the Col du Pis on the west. The peaks of Balsille are fringed with pines, but the rocks themselves are so pointed and broken that they resemble tops of pines on a Titan scale. There are four principal peaks, and so the mountain has been named Quatre Dents." The term château, or castle, used in this narrative was applied to a kind of grassy platform at the top.

CHAPTER XI.

Although the Vaudois were not wholly despoiled of the fruit of their heroic efforts in fighting their way back to their native valleys, yet the cruel banishment of the French Protestants, and the removal of so many of their gifted and devoted leaders, was a very heavy calamity. It placed almost insuperable difficulties in the way of their reorganization. Furthermore, they were greatly harassed by the imposition of taxes far beyond their means, and most unjustly levied *only* on the Protestants. Very dishonourable attempts were also made to seduce their children from the profession of evangelical principles. They were not allowed to repair their shattered temples, and were deprived of a proper number of pastors; so that altogether they were in an evil case. Their proverbial and long-tried loyalty to their prince, however, flourished in spite of these discouragements. Victor Amadeus, having joined England and Holland against France, was besieged in Turin by the latter power in 1706. He was so hardly pressed by the French troops as to be obliged to take refuge among his faithful subjects of the valleys. A family named Durand had the honour of giving shelter to their fugitive prince; and when by the forced marches of Prince Eugene deliverance was at hand, King Amadeus conferred the right of burying in their own garden on the family which sheltered him, as well as bequeathed his own silver spoons and drinking-cup to the family. I had the pleasure of seeing one of these spoons, preserved in the museum at La Torre, on the occasion of my visit in 1871. Eugene and the Duke of Savoy ascended the heights of the Superga (a hill about six miles from Turin) together. The prince, detecting some mistakes in the movements of the French troops, exclaimed, "It seems to me that these people are already half beaten;" whereupon the duke vowed, if Turin were delivered from the French, that he would erect a monument on that spot to the Virgin. He kept his vow, and the present imposing structure, used as a mausoleum for the House of Savoy, was begun in 1717, and finished fourteen years after. But he was not equally mindful of his obligations to his devoted Vaudois, who, in addition to protecting their prince at the risk of their own safety, also inflicted great injury upon the French troops when obliged to raise the siege of Turin. Indeed the vexations to which the Vaudois were subjected by the interference of the French court as the ready instrument of papal cruelty and intolerance provoked the kindly interposition of Frederick I. of Prussia on their behalf. However, Amadeus would not protect the converts from Catholicism, although he was firm in maintaining the rights of the Vaudois within the narrow limits which had been conceded. Still these faithful subjects of the House of Savoy had to bear many grievous acts of injustice, from which they were exempted by the express words of the royal edicts. However, they endured all these irritations from papal lawlessness without being led away by the seductive promises and the illusory hopes of freedom and happiness which so largely unsettled the continent of Europe by the outbreak of the French Revolution in 1789. Indeed so sensitive were they of anything which might bring their loyalty into question that they actually suspended one of their pastors from his functions for six months because he had inadvertently alluded to revolutionary principles from his pulpit! I may add that the same principle of wise abstention from all political discussions still characterize the Vaudois pastors, both in the valleys and the mission-field of the Italian peninsula.

In the wars between France and Savoy at this time the Vaudois had the guardianship of the frontiers entrusted to them. In 1793 the French tried hard to move the Vaudois from their fidelity by the most attractive promises of civil and religious liberty. Although they refused to listen to these promises, yet the ready tongue of calumny took advantage of circumstances connected with the surrender of the fort of Mirabocco to asperse their integrity. Investigation showed that if Musset (the only Vaudois officer present at the time) had been in command, the place would have been defended to the last. Still such was the spirit engendered by popish fanaticism, that a most frightful conspiracy to murder the defenceless Vaudois women and children of San Giovanni and La Torre, while their fathers and brothers were all away guarding the frontiers, was concocted. Happily for the credit of Christianity and humanity it was discovered and revealed in time by two members of the Romish faith, who were too honourable to sanction such a scheme. These gentlemen, Brianza, priest of Lucerna, and Captain Odetti, gave notice to the Vaudois. Messengers were at once despatched to the mountains. General Gaudin at first refused to let them go to the defence of their homes, disbelieving the existence of the conspiracy until he was shown the names of seven hundred of those engaged in it. Then he hesitated to weaken his forces against the French; but a stratagem happily relieved him of his embarrassment, though eventually he lost his command for his humanity, *while none of the conspirators were punished!* Instead of this a Vaudois captain, Davit, was executed, and others placed under arrest upon unjust suspicions. By these proceedings a feeling of disquietude was provoked, which only the appointment of General Zimmerman, a native of Lucerna, was able to calm.

An armistice taking place in the spring of 1796, and Charles Emmanuel IV. coming to the Sardinian crown, the British ambassador sought more considerate treatment of the Vaudois. In reply to this appeal they were allowed to repair and enlarge their temples, and even to remove them to more commodious sites. In 1798 Charles Emmanuel IV. was only allowed the island of Sardinia by the all-conquering French, who took possession of Piedmont, and annexed it as a province to France. This event gave to the Vaudois in a moment every social right, every political privilege, and, above all, the religious freedom they had for centuries fought, and bled, and suffered in vain to procure, at least in its entirety!

However, the position of the Vaudois was one of difficulty. Under the rule of their *de facto* government they took part in repressing the uprising of the Piedmontese against the French at Carmagnola. And when three hundred wounded soldiers, fleeing from the Austrian army, who pursued them to the Vaudois frontiers, reached Bobbio in a state of appalling destitution, M. Rostaing, the pastor, and his people, fed them out of their scanty stores, dressed their wounds, and carried them on their shoulders over frightful precipices, and along snow-covered defiles impassable to ordinary traffic. This act of humanity (gratefully acknowledged by the French commander, Suchet) would have drawn upon them a fresh outpouring of oppression, had not the Russian general taken a truer estimate of their position. He allowed them to retain their arms on the condition that they used them only in self-defence. Napoleon's victory at Marengo, on the 14th June, 1800, consolidated the French rule over Piedmont. But the Vaudois experienced dreadful privations at this time, owing to the ravages of the soldiers of the two armies, French and Austrian, and a period of scarcity. The stipends of the pastors were also in great part wanting. The French government made a provision out of appropriations formerly given to the Romish priests and monks. Indeed, after a conversation which Napoleon held in a most agreeable manner with M. Peyrani, moderator of the Vaudois Church, he assigned stipends of one thousand francs yearly to the pastors of parishes, together with an extra allowance of two hundred francs for work as secretaries of the communes. On this occasion Napoleon referred in a spirit of admiration to the exploits of Arnaud and other brave leaders of the Vaudois, and also drew from M. Peyrani the statement that his church had an independent existence from about the year 820. At this time the Vaudois rebuilt their temple at Giovanni, closed since the year 1658. However, it was barely finished when it suffered much damage from an earthquake, the shocks of which were felt for a period of four months in the neighbourhood of Pinerolo, and in other parts, both of Italy and France. Although the prevalence of this earthquake inflicted great suffering on the Vaudois by the cessation of all industrial pursuits, the necessity of living in tents, and the general terror and alarm which it inspired, yet the actual loss of life did not extend to more than three cases. There were many remarkable deliverances. Notwithstanding this visitation of Providence, it does not appear that religious life existed to the degree of former times. The spirit of atheism stirred up in France; the prevalence of a cold materialistic philosophy in those seminaries where the students for the Waldensian ministry had to seek instruction; the absorption of the thoughts by the reports of military expeditions; the bewitchery attached to the name and achievements of Bonaparte, not only made the young men of the valleys willing to enrol beneath his standard, but also had a tendency to restrict the simplicity and the piety so characteristic of their forefathers to those who from sex or age were left outside of that turbid wave which swept others into the current of its power. In 1815 came the downfall of the proud empire erected by the military prowess and boundless ambition of the first Napoleon. How this affected the Vaudois we will consider in our next chapter.

CHAPTER XII.

On the return of Victor Emmanuel I. to the throne of his fathers, with augmented dominions, the Waldenses had such favourable expectations from his knowledge of them that out of respect to his feelings they abstained from certain efforts which they might have used at the congress of Vienna for the preservation of their rights. Unhappily, these hopes were not realized. The king passed an edict restricting the Vaudois to the concessions enjoyed before the French occupation; and in place of the stipend of one thousand francs for their pastors he assigned them only half the amount. The Romish priests, not content with the restoration of the infamous hospital for abducting Protestant children at Pinerolo, and other grants made by the French, actually set up a claim for income which had accrued during the period of their dispossession. This, however, Count Crotti, superintendent of the province, refused, on the ground that the Vaudois administered not only lawfully, but in such a way as to enhance rather than diminish the value of the property. The temple of Giovanni was also closed again, but only for one year, though the use of it was accompanied by an injunction to place a screen before the entrance, so as to mollify the opposition of the priest of the Romish chapel exactly opposite in the same village. The king further allowed the Vaudois to retain property outside the valleys acquired during the French occupation; also to follow, besides ordinary trades, the professions of surgeon, apothecary, and architect.

As the old machinery of fire and sword was no longer available, the enemies of the Vaudois sought to win them from their principles by the issue of pastoral letters from the bishops of Pinerolo. Messrs. Bigez, Rey, and Charvaz engaged in these attempts, but without success, the pastors refuting their epistles, especially MM. Geymet, Rodolph, Peyran, and Mondon. Victor Emmanuel having abdicated in 1821, was succeeded by Carlo Felice, a bigoted Romanist. He published a decree for restricting the liberties of the Vaudois according to the terms of the edict of 1622. He also allowed a bull of Pope Gregory, which forbids "to those of the pretended reformed religion" the right of trading among the Romanists. By means, however, of protests from the representatives of England and Prussia this last act of tyranny was not persevered in. Still, when the Waldenses asked to see their king, he denied them audience in the following terms: "Tell them they only want one thing; that is, to be Catholics." Their loyalty, indeed, was conspicuous; for they stood almost alone in 1821, when the rest of Piedmont was wavering in its fidelity to the house of Savoy. In 1831 Carlo Alberto ascended the throne. Although greatly under the influence of the Church of Rome, he yet showed a spirit of justice towards his Vaudois subjects. For instance, he not only removed the disability by which they were denied an officer's commission in the Sardinian army, but on the occasion of the death of Major Bonnet, a Vaudois in his service, who had been buried without the honours due to his rank, he commanded that the body should be exhumed and removed to La Torre at his expense, and there be interred with all the respect due to the aged soldier. He further settled an annuity upon the major's children. Something of this same alternation between subjection to Rome and the aspirations of justice showed itself in another transaction of his reign, namely, that of the erection of a church and priory for the accommodation of eight missionary fathers of the order of St. Maurice and Lazarus at La Torre. These buildings stand at the very entrance of the town as you approach from Giovanni. I confess their presence suggested disagreeable thoughts to my mind. They seemed so out of harmony with the spirit of the new era of justice and freedom, and to awaken so many memories of past oppressions. But these thoughts were as nothing to the gloomy apprehensions which actually filled the minds of the Vaudois at the date of their erection. They were not a little perplexed, beside, as to the way in which they should act on the occasion of the visit of their king to attend the ceremonial of this church consecration. However, a gracious Providence interposed on their behalf, and showed the character of their sovereign in an assuring light. First of all he sent back the troops of the line which were proposed as his escort. Instead of these he consented to be received by the militia of the valleys, stating, in reply to those who urged a guard of regular troops, "I require no guard in the midst of the Vaudois." The king was most cordially welcomed, and, being deeply touched by his reception, ordered each company of the militia to pass before him according to their communes, and with their respective colours. He also gave an audience to the Vaudois Table, left money to be distributed among the poor, in which the Protestants shared; and to perpetuate the memory of this visit of September 24th, 1844, caused a fountain to be erected close by with the inscription, "Il re Carolo Alberto, al popolo che l'accoglieva con tanto affetto." "The king Charles Albert to the people who welcomed him with so much affection."

This pleasing episode in the history of the Vaudois forms a fitting prelude to the advent of a yet more substantial token of good-will on the part of their sovereign. I mean that edict of emancipation which, while it did justice to the people of the valleys, also, by the circumstances of their inclusion, made the kingdom of Sardinia a true pattern of constitutional monarchy; kept her true amidst the perfidy and violence by which the sovereigns of other states withdrew on the morrow the boon of the yesterday, and in consequence reaped a harvest of anarchy and disorder; while brave Piedmont has not only remained firm as a rock, but has been gathering to itself, one by one, the minute subdivisions of the Italian peninsula, until at length we see its true and faithful sovereign, "il Re galantuomo," the monarch of all that stretches from the Tyrol on the north to Sicily on the south. "His sceptre rules and banner waves" from the shore of the Adriatic to the valleys of the Alps. And throughout the length and breadth of that land, whilst neighbouring countries, notably those most servile to the papacy, Spain and France, have been convulsed by terrors and paralysed by intestine and foreign wars, the tricoloured flag of the Italian kingdom floats triumphantly above the walls of ancient Rome, and such an era of peaceful contentment and commercial enterprise has begun as its proud cities and luxuriant plains have long been strangers to. Just as with regard to God's Israel of the East, so does it seem to have been with this modern Israel of the West. The nations who persecuted and despoiled the sons of Abraham have been despoiled themselves. The nations who befriended the Jews have risen to power and influence. Likewise the persecutors of God's faithful ones in the valleys of the Po, notably the priest-king and France, have been scourged; whilst the countries which befriended them in their long series of trials, the Protestant states of Germany, Holland, and our own land, have been distinguished by a constantly augmenting prosperity. Oh, that men were wise! Oh, that politicians would remember that it is righteousness which exalteth a nation. The thought that Piedmont became the Zoar of the living Church of God, when its members fled from the Sodom of pagan and papal persecution and corruption, is not one of the least of the grounds of hope, that not only shall its political expansion continue, but that with it shall also be united that nobler gift of the gospel of Christ, in its purity and power conveying the glorious liberty of the children of God to the millions who have so long groaned beneath the bondage of Antichrist.

But these thoughts remind us that the precious boon of emancipation for the Vaudois did not descend upon them without an intervening period of doubt and struggle.

The political changes first announced in October, 1847, did not include the Vaudois within their range. Hence they had to ask for a special act by which their freedom should be conceded. All the liberals supported this demand. At a banquet at Pinerolo, Audifredi, an advocate, said, "Twenty thousand of our brothers stand, so to speak, enclosed and isolated between two torrents in our delightful valleys. They are honourable, laborious, strong in mind and body, equal to other Italians. With enlightened dispositions and by severe sacrifices they have educated their children, but oppressed by burdens they do not enjoy the rights of other citizens. To us it belongs, as their nearest brethren, to vote that by an universal brotherhood there shall no longer be the embankment of these torrents, that the country should be their mother and not their stepmother, and that as they are judged suitable to defend their country by the arm, so it should be allowed that they can enlighten and elevate it by the mind. *Evviva la emancipazione dei Valdesi.*"[F]

An immense petition was drawn up, headed by the names of Marquis Roberto d'Azeglio, Count Cavour, Cesare Balbo, and, strange to say, the Bishop of Pinerolo. The attorney-general, Count Sclopis, supported the memorial, because, said he, by careful examination of the criminal records of the government, "no other population of the country could be compared with the Vaudois in morality and virtue." At length the *statuto* was published in the *Official Gazette* on the 25th of February, 1848 (though dated the 17th of that month). On the evening of that day the residences of the English and Prussian ambassadors were brilliantly illuminated, as likewise the houses of nearly all the Protestants in Turin. Moreover, the news of this happy event soon spread itself over the valleys. At nightfall some hundreds of bonfires were kindled on the hills, and even upon the tops, yet crowned with snow, and thus the joyous demonstrations of the Protestants of the capital were united in by their brethren on the hill sides.

But two days after this there was a yet greater demonstration of gladness. Deputations from all parts of the kingdom met in Turin to express their united thanks to their monarch for the constitution bestowed upon his people. The Vaudois assembled in large numbers, and, with the Protestants inhabiting the city, formed a column of more than six hundred persons, headed by ten pastors, and bearing aloft a magnificent banner of the colours of Savoy, on which was written, embroidered in large silver letters, these simple but expressive words—

"A RE CARLO ALBERTO I., VALDESI RICONOSCENTI."

(The grateful Waldenses to Charles Albert.)[G] While the large procession was waiting to start, a deputation was sent to the Vaudois, begging that they would take the place of honour. "Vaudois," they said, "until now you have been the last; to-day justice must be done you, and you shall walk at our head!" And so it was. The Vaudois column, preceded by its banner, and surrounded by twelve children, dressed in the Italian costume of the sixteenth century, opened the march; and then a spectacle unknown in the annals of Piedmont was displayed in the capital, and by it to the kingdom. In every street wherever the procession traversed, wherever appeared the flag of the persecuted Church, hands clapped, handkerchiefs waved, hats (even that of a priest) rose in the air, "Evviva ái Valdesi! Evviva l'emancipazione!" burst from thousands of mouths, and many of the spectators, leaving the ranks, came and hung upon the neck of some member of the column, accompanying the act (sufficiently expressive in itself) by words of a most affecting and brotherly character. The enthusiasm was indescribable. What a contrast between the acclamations of that day and the cries of "Death to the heretic!" which in other times these same streets so often heard at the passing of some confessor of the gospel to a cruel death![H]

What these festive proceedings foreshadowed as to the extension and deepening of the piety and power of the church of the valleys must be reserved for our next chapter.

FOOTNOTES:

[F] *Gli Evangelici Valdesi*, per PAOLO GEYMONAT, Professore di Teologia in Firenze.

[G] This banner was afterwards presented to the king, and most graciously received by him.

[H] *Le General Beckwith, sa vie a ses travaux*. By J. P. MEILLE, Pasteur.

CHAPTER XIII.

We concluded our last amidst the gladness of heart which filled the souls of myriads to whom social progress, political freedom, and evangelical truth were precious. Our object now is to recount the fruits of that enlargement accorded to the Vaudois; and in order to do this we must take a retrospect of their religious condition for some few years before the arrival of that grand epoch. At that period the state of things in the valleys was far from satisfactory. Not to recount, as among the causes, those political disabilities to which reference has been previously made, I will refer to some additional circumstances of a vexatious and depressing character. One was the hindrances to the obtaining the most indispensable religious books, such as Bibles, catechisms, hymn-books. With each parcel of Bibles and New Testaments, the moderator was obliged to sign a formal undertaking that not a single copy should be sold, nor even lent to a Roman Catholic. Again, in all the communes of the valleys, where nearly all the proprietors were Protestants, and scarcely a Roman Catholic could be found who was not either living on alms or employed as a daily labourer, the law required that the *majority* of the members of the communal council should be always and necessarily composed of Romanists.

As regards primary education, the valleys were more favourably circumstanced than other parts of the kingdom. Out of a population of some twenty thousand, nearly four thousand attended school, at least during the winter months. However, it will be seen that the real work of education was not in so satisfactory a condition as the above statement, in a superficial point of view, might imply. To show this we will descend to details as to the schools, their kind, structure, fittings, and teachers.

First, then, we take the HAMLET SCHOOLS, about one hundred and twenty in number. They were carried on generally in a *stable*, and the place was neither remarkable for space nor cleanliness; so that on one side, in a narrow division, would be thirty or forty children, separated from the sheep or the goats by so slender a space that not infrequently the heads of the children and the animals would combine in a way more grotesque than effective for educational purposes.

The amount of didactic efficiency to be expected in the teacher may be surmised from the circumstance of his salary being sometimes less than the munificent sum of threepence-halfpenny per day! With such machinery we may feel it was an achievement to be grateful for, if by the end of the winter's session the children had learnt to read, write, and cipher moderately, and could repeat by heart a prayer for morning and evening, the Lord's Prayer, the Decalogue, and the Apostles' Creed.

Second. There were also the PARISH SCHOOLS, open ten months in the year, and attended during the winter by a large number of children, the majority of whom had to leave on the advent of spring to work in the fields. Those not so required remained in the district or hamlet schools. The buildings in which the parish schools were conducted were not exactly stables, but yet entirely destitute of the light, air, fittings, and furniture requisite for school-work. The only reading-books were a French Bible and Italian acts of parliament. So much, then, for the primary schools. The condition of the *secondary or grammar schools* was not much more encouraging. The institution was migratory, and aimed to teach fifteen or twenty pupils, divided into five classes, under one teacher, not always very competent, and badly paid, as much Latin and Greek as would secure their admission as students in the academies of Strasbourg, Lausanne, or Geneva. But we pass from schools to things religious and ecclesiastical. Morals were comparatively pure; there was a respect for religion; a frequent attendance on public worship; a deep attachment to their ancestral faith; a disposition to endure everything rather than deny it; and affection and esteem for their pastors. As regards the pastors, they were, almost without exception, faithful to the ancient evangelical orthodoxy.

But there was that which both pastors and flocks were very imperfectly acquainted with, viz., on one side the aim and mission of the church, and on the other the true nature of the fruits intended to be produced by the preaching of the gospel. In a word, there was a lack of true spiritual energy, a realization of the need and preciousness of salvation. There was the outward shell of orthodoxy, but the living soul of godliness was wanting. Jesus Christ was present in name, but absent in reality.

In the administration of the church there were many serious defects. The meeting of the synods was very difficult, partly because of the suspicions of the government, and partly from the unwillingness of the communes to bear the expense connected therewith. Again, the synods themselves answered but imperfectly to the design of their institution, and their influence on the spiritual state of the church very small. The Table, in its turn, forgetting that its duties were essentially religious, sunk insensibly into a kind of higher tribunal for secular affairs. The same tendency showed itself in the bosom of the consistories.

However, amidst these deep shades some gleams of light, the heralds of better things, began to show themselves. The first of these hopeful signs was due to the liberality, as regards its beginning, of Madame Geymet, who in the year 1826 laid the foundation of a hospital for the poor Waldensians at La Torre. Madame Geymet was encouraged warmly by Pastor La Bert, the then moderator of the Waldensian Church, and Pastor Cellerier, of Geneva, who made a collection in aid of the object. The Count Waldburg Truchsesse,

Prussian ambassador at Turin, obtained help from Prussia; Dr. Gilly, by means of the committee in London, sent large help from this country. Holland, France, and Russia also joined in the effort; so that at length the brave projector had the satisfaction of seeing *two* hospitals grow out of her once ridiculed scheme. The second hospital was erected at Pomaret, for the especial benefit of the valleys of San Martino and Pragela.

Another means of awakening at this time arose from the arrival of some young ministers, who had just left the foreign academies, especially that of Lausanne, where the influence of a spiritual revival had been particularly felt. A visit paid to the different parishes of the valleys in 1826 by Felix Neff and Pastor Blanc, of Mens, resulted in much spiritual fruit.

These were but streaks of morning light, however. Long years had to pass, and many painful struggles to be engaged in, before the Sun of Righteousness shone clearly with His beneficent rays on the thick woods and the shady corners of these lovely valleys. Among those who have been the means of promoting the revival of true religion in the Waldensian Church stand out conspicuously the names of Dr. Gilly and General Beckwith. The former paid his first visit to the valleys in 1823. As that visit became the germ of so much blessing to the Vaudois, it is not unimportant to recall the providential circumstance which led to that visit. Referring to the doctor's own narrative,[1] he says, "I happened to attend a meeting of the Society for Promoting Christian Knowledge on a day when a very affecting letter was read to the board, signed Ferdinand Peyrani, minister of Pramol, 'and requested that some aid might be sent, in books or money, to the ancient Protestant congregation in the mountains of Piedmont, who were struggling hard against poverty and oppression.'" The society voted forty pounds' worth of books, including those mentioned as specially needed for use in their churches. But from the date of this incident Dr. Gilly sought after fuller information respecting the Vaudois, and determined on visiting their valleys. This purpose he carried into effect early in the year 1823, and on his return home the next year he published an account of his journey, his object being to excite an *immediate* interest on behalf of these people. How largely he succeeded, so as to entitle him to be reckoned among their chiefest benefactors, we shall have occasion to remark later on. But, apart from the formation of a large and influential committee in London, by which considerable sums of money were raised "to assist the Vaudois in maintaining their ministers, churches, schools, and poor," he was the means of invoking the sympathy and aid of one who consecrated his life, strength, and means in one almost unbroken series of efforts for their amelioration— I mean General Beckwith. This distinguished philanthropist was born at Halifax, Nova Scotia, October 2nd, 1789. He was baptized by the names of John Charles, and entered the 95th Regiment in the year 1803. His first years as a soldier were spent in Hanover, Denmark, and Sweden. In 1809 he was engaged in the Peninsular War, being present at the disastrous retreat from Corunna and the sieges of Salamanca and Toulouse. For his services at the last place he received a gold medal and the rank of major, March 3rd, 1814. During these campaigns he was never wounded, although exposed to great danger. One morning, among others, his old servant had scarcely reached the skirts of a forest in which the enemy had an ambuscade than his master's horse was killed by a ball, and the rider overthrown. The servant thought it was all over with his master, but the sad thought had hardly entered his mind when Beckwith sprang up and cried out, "All right, John," and by a quick movement escaped beyond reach of the enemy's fire.

On the return of Napoleon from Elba, Beckwith rejoined the standard of Wellington, and took a prominent part in the battle of Waterloo. On this day he had four horses killed under him, but received no personal injury until he was struck by a cannon ball in the left leg from the retreating fire of the French. After three months' unsuccessful treatment amputation was declared necessary. This random shot, like the bow drawn at a venture in an ancient battle, was pregnant with mighty consequences, not only to Beckwith personally, but to that interesting people to whom as yet he had never given a thought.

Beckwith, though only twenty-six years of age, was made a lieutenant-colonel on the field of battle, and received the silver medal struck to commemorate the victory. Had he not lost his leg he would probably have risen to the highest distinction as a soldier. But if so he might never have become the instrument of such extensive blessings to the Vaudois as was destined in the providence of God.

The first foundation stone, so to speak, on which was to be erected the spacious superstructure of his after benevolence began at the time of his retirement to the château of Mont St. Jean, during the period of weakness resulting from his wound at Waterloo. The owner of the mansion had a little girl, six years of age, who was a most attentive nurse to him. She hardly ever left his bedside, and by her childish prattling, innocent pleasantries, and tender sympathy, won his regard, and spread a charm over a time of pain and depression; so much so, indeed, that when the time of separation came it greatly distressed him, and in after life he never spoke of her without evident emotion.

But it was in this way God led him first to that benevolent interest in the young which afterwards became so marked a feature of his character.

But up to this time, whilst Beckwith was not a sceptic, yet his faith was not of an operative kind, he was taken up with those pursuits which belonged solely to time. The means employed by God to awaken him to a knowledge of the real aim of life was a copy of His own Word. This treasure had lain unused at the bottom of his portmanteau until he lay wounded at a little village near Courtray, in Belgium. Then he began to read with an interest not previously felt, and it became to him the word of life. When he was questioned about the circumstances of his conversion, he used to reply, in his graphic way: "The good God said, 'Stop here, you rascal!' and He has cut off my leg, and I think I shall be the more happy without it."

Of Beckwith's character as a soldier one of his former companions writes thus: "I always regarded Beckwith as an officer of very brilliant promise, for he embodied all the requisites of a great commander: remarkable quickness in conception, imperturbable coolness in the time of action, admirable power of organization, with indomitable courage. When he was major he always left a position of safety to mix in the thick of the fight, and I remember meeting him in the breach of Ciudad Rodrigo at the head of an attacking column when he might have been in the rear." The same person also testifies to Beckwith's care of his men, extending even to minute particulars about clothing. Also, that he was a great favourite with his brother officers on account of his intelligence and amiability. After recovering somewhat from his wound he returned to England, and visited America during this time. Shortly after his arrival in England from the latter place he sought out his old companions in the army, and among others he called on the Duke of Wellington.

It was while calling at Apsley House on one of these occasions he was shown into the library, and whilst waiting a short time for the duke his eye fell upon a number of new books, including *Dr. Gilly's Visit to the Vaudois*. On leaving he obtained a copy of the book. The result was that he determined to visit the valleys himself, which event happened in the autumn of 1827.

Owing to the weather he stayed only a few days, but returned the following year, and continued his visits to the valleys year after year, until, in 1833, a severe illness obliged him to remain in England. In the autumn of 1835 he returned, and lived in the valleys with Pastor Bonjour, at St. John's, for the next five years. Again, after an interval of two years, he returned to the valleys, living at the ancient castle of La Torre. In 1836 the Vaudois Table had his portrait painted, and engravings distributed through the valleys. In 1844 the synod presented him with a cup of honour, also Dr. Gilly and the Count Waldburg Truchsesse. In 1846 he was promoted to the rank of major-general in the English army, and also received the dignity of a Knight of St. Maurice and Lazarus from the king of Sardinia. In 1850 he married a Vaudoise. In 1862 he dies among the people he had so long loved and served, and is buried at La Torre, amid the profoundest grief and deepest veneration of the whole population.

FOOTNOTES:

[1] *Narrative of an Excursion to the Mountains of Piedmont in the year 1823.* By WILLIAM STEPHEN GILLY. 2nd Ed. C. and J. Rivington.

CHAPTER XIV.

Our last chapter closed with a brief sketch of the life of Beckwith, so that in the present I might be free to speak of the work done, without interpolations as to the personal movements of him who was in several respects the chief worker. To those who desire to read the full particulars of General Beckwith's life, I very earnestly commend the deeply interesting work of Pastor J. P. Meille, to whose pages I am greatly indebted.

Beckwith was early impressed with the conviction that God had providentially preserved the Vaudois, that they might be the agents of evangelizing Italy, through the political changes which were being wrought in that country by means of the kingdom of Sardinia. He was the first to recognize this important truth, and he never lost sight of it, either in the motive which it supplied for his own efforts, or in the influence he sought to bring to bear upon others. This belief in the mission of the Vaudois quickened all his sympathies and guided all his plans. To turn to these plans, one of the earliest was the improvement and extension of primary education. Beckwith saw at once the value of the Quartier schools, and he began to erect a better class of buildings for this purpose. First of all he bore the whole expense, excepting the site; afterwards he paid the cost of labour in erecting the buildings, but required the inhabitants to supply material as well as site. He also oftentimes contributed largely to augment the salary of the underpaid teachers. Some one hundred and twenty buildings, commodious and well-situated, were the result of these efforts.

But the improvement in the hamlet schools brought out more distinctly the sad condition of the parish schools. To overcome difficulties, Beckwith would say to the parish authorities, You need a better school and residence for your teacher; if you will raise a thousand francs (about a fourth or fifth, according to circumstances), I will supply the rest.

If this offer was accepted, the colonel generally made the contract, and overlooked the erection of the building.

In this way, a little by little, some this year and others the next, in nearly every commune of the valleys there rose up commodious edifices, duly furnished with all the requisites of teaching. The change was immense from the narrow, confined, ill-ventilated, badly lighted, and unfurnished buildings which had previously existed.

The reformation, however, in the buildings and their fittings was not the only thing requisite for a good school. Good teachers were also needed, and to procure these it was necessary to augment the scale of stipend. At the time under review the highest salary was from three to four hundred francs (£12 or £16) per annum. Beckwith set about this task, and being ably supported by the moderator of the church, M. Bonjour, he had the satisfaction of seeing an arrangement made by which the salaries of the teachers were raised one-third. This augmentation began on the 1st of January, 1837. But the good effected by this movement was not simply the increased pay of the teacher; it raised the work in public estimation, and gave to the teacher's position a degree of security which enabled him to devote himself more entirely to teaching as a distinct profession.

Another means for advancing education was that of increasing the personal efficiency of the teachers themselves. To accomplish this, the teachers of all the parish schools in the valleys were sent for a course of instruction at the normal college at Lausanne. The expense of this important measure was borne entirely by Beckwith. And, moreover, to secure permanently the above results, a rule was adopted by the synod in 1839, that henceforth every teacher in the Vaudois parish schools must produce a certificate of didactic power, as well as moral fitness for the office.

Beckwith's next movement was the establishment of a boarding-school for girls. I had the pleasure of visiting this very interesting and important institution in 1871, and was struck by the efficiency and excellence of its character. But it is time to refer to his exertions in connection with SECONDARY instruction. Although Dr. Gilly very deservedly has the chief credit in reference to the erection of that noble college of the Holy Trinity at La Torre, which forms so imposing and interesting an object to the Christian tourist, and which constituted so marked an epoch in the restoration of piety and sound learning among the pastors and general population of the valleys, yet it must be acknowledged that the many difficulties associated with this grand enterprise would hardly have been surmounted, had it not have been for the presence on the spot of so true a friend to the Vaudois, and so able an ally of the noble projector of the college, as his military colleague.

Not only did he provide a building for the grammar school whose location had been one of the difficulties connected with the establishment of the college, but he also superintended the erection of the buildings, and gave a sum of ten thousand francs towards the cost. Dr. Gilly acknowledges these things in a letter to the moderator under date of April 28th, 1835. He also was instrumental, with Dr. Gilly, in founding a grammar school at Pomaret. This school was subsequently enlarged by the efforts of the Rev. Dr. Stewart, of Leghorn, another warm-hearted friend of the Waldensian Church.

In 1847 Beckwith erected a group of houses, just above the college, for the residence of the professors. But important as were the reformations sought and obtained in the educational machinery of the valleys, yet it was almost as needful to improve the character of the ecclesiastical edifices used by the Vaudois. Few were such as fitted the purposes to which they were set apart. There is nothing surprising in this when we consider the circumstances of the Vaudois through so many centuries. But, easy as it is to account for the lack of edifices appropriate to the decent and reverent worship of Almighty God at the period referred to, the thing itself was nevertheless a misfortune. Hence in 1843 Beckwith offered to restore the temple at Rodoret, which was in a most deplorable state. The temple was not alone in its need; the parsonage-house, a very crazy building, was destroyed by an avalanche on the 16th of January, 1845, burying beneath its ruins the pastor, his wife, their little child, aged five months, and servant, the only living creature escaping being the pastor's dog! The new temple being finished in March, Beckwith commenced operations for the erection of a suitable presbytery. The total cost of the new building was thirteen thousand francs, contributed chiefly by Beckwith, but with the help of the commune, Dr. Stewart, of Leghorn, and friends in Dublin and America.

His next work was the restoration of the church at Rora. This matter was accompanied by a pleasing incident. He was speaking of the affair at the house of a friend in England. A little girl of the family overheard the conversation, and, approaching the general, offered him a penny, saying she would like to assist in building the church. He was much touched by this action of the child, and taking her on his knees, said, "Yes, my friend; with that which you have given me I will build the church; and your penny, placed in the corner stone, will tell all the world that you have been the founder." The new building was consecrated in January, 1846. Other temples and presbyteries were restored, including that of Prali. The churches of Coppier and Angrogna were restored in 1847 by Mrs. General Molyneux Williams. But a greater work was accomplished in 1852, when Beckwith erected a church for the parish of La Torre, which, under the influence of oppressive edicts, had been deprived of its temple for hundreds of years. This edifice is, both as regards dimensions and architecture, suited to the position it holds as the parish church of the capital of the valleys; those valleys no longer dreading the approach of sanguinary bands to pillage and destroy, its people no longer crushed beneath a bondage which refused them the opportunities of worship in their own parochial boundaries according to the creed and ritual of their sainted and heroic forefathers. This grand work was the last preliminary to that church extension and missionary revival which the era of emancipation made possible to the Vaudois Church, and which Beckwith had so long eagerly and clearly anticipated.

CHAPTER XV.

The first exercise of evangelical liberty accorded to the Vaudois Church was shown in the attempt to preach the gospel and establish a place of Protestant worship, at what, in point of geographical nearness, was the neighbouring city, but not in the past the *neighbourly* city of Pinerolo. The work was, however, accomplished chiefly by the munificence of American Protestants. Then came the opening of the edifice, which so worthily represents the Vaudois cause in Turin. Beckwith took a very energetic part in this important work. But the actual modern mission work of the Vaudois Church may be said to have begun in May, 1849, when Professor Malan preached in the temple at St. Giovanni (for the first time for centuries past) the gospel in the Italian language.

The Count Guiccardini and some other persons of social position at Florence and its neighbourhood joined the Vaudois Church in 1850. The same year a Vaudois missionary was appointed to Turin, chiefly by the liberality of two English gentlemen, Messrs. Brewin and Milsom. In 1851 a great many refugees, for conscience' sake, from Florence (the result of evangelistic labours there), fled to Turin and swelled the numbers of the Vaudois congregation.

Also on the evening of the day on which was laid the foundation of the new temple, Mazzarella, a Neapolitan advocate, deputy of parliament, and judge of the court of appeal at Genoa, was one of ten catechumens received into the membership of the Vaudois Church.

At the same time the gospel was finding its way into Genoa, a city devoted to Mariolatry. On the very day on which the Table decided to send M. Geymonat from Turin to work in Genoa, they received an application by letter from Genoa to admit to their communion and ministry a very distinguished ex-priest of Rome. This was no other than Dr. De Sanctis, rector of the Magdalen and professor of theology, &c., at Rome. Excepting during a short period, to which I need not refer, the connection thus begun between Dr. De Sanctis and the Vaudois continued until his lamented death on the last day of December, 1869. But there are two points I will allude to. First, the incidental means of his conversion. This was by a little treatise put into his hands at a time when he was preparing a series of lectures in defence of the decrees of the Council of Trent as compared with the word of God.

Secondly, the ground on which he sought admission into the Vaudois Church. In the letter addressed to the Table, dated August 17th, 1852, he states that he had abandoned the Church of Rome for nearly five years, and from the moment of his separation until then his thoughts "always turned to the Church of the Valleys, *because he recognized it as the true, primitive, apostolic*

Italian Church." "During these five years," he adds, "I have lived among Christians who have proposed to me many times, with a view to my temporal advantage, that I should join some church; but I have always refused, thinking that *an Italian, sincerely seeking the good of his compatriots, should not belong to any other church than the ancient Italian Church.*" I have transcribed these words, because I feel strongly their importance as coming from one so well able to estimate the value of the Vaudois in its past history and its adaptation to the necessities and opportunities of evangelizing that country so much needing the gospel of Christ—the Italy of to-day. It seems to me that it is for this very purpose that the little community confined within so narrow a space, apart from the more populous and frequented parts of Europe, has been preserved, in spite of so many attempts at extermination. What the seven thousand who did not bow the knee to Baal were to the rest of Israel, so it would seem that the faithful few in the valleys of Piedmont are intended to be in reference to that new kingdom of Italy, of which they form one of the most ancient provinces. And the whole attitude and character of the Church of the Valleys confirms this feeling. They can appeal to their brother Italians as no foreigners can. Their very sufferings give them a right which cannot be ignored. Mazzarella eloquently acknowledged this when he visited La Torre. Again, by the removal of their college to Florence; their literary enterprise in such publications as the *Amico di Casa, Amico Dei Fanculli, La Rivista Christiana*; the talent, zeal, and organizing power of their missionary agency, they show themselves fully alive to the privileged responsibilities of their position in Italy, and fully entitled to the hearty confidence and liberal support of all who desire the supremacy of evangelic truth in that land which has been so long the head quarters of the papacy!

The following statement of agencies will confirm my assertion:—

DISTRICT.	STATION.	AGENTS.	Pastors.	Evangelists.	Communicants.	Day Scholars.	Sunday Scholars.
PIEDMONT	Susa	Sig. A. Castioni	..	1	14	0	..
,,	Courmayeur	Sig. F. Costabel	..	1	17	15	..
,,	Aosta and Vallata	Sig. S. Girardone	..	1	19	11	9
,,	Ivrea and neighbourhood } Castelrosso-Verolengo	Rev. Daniel Revel	1	..	70	..	15
,,	Pietra Marazzi	Sig. T. Pugno	..	1	24	6	4
,,	Monte Castello } Pecetto	Sig. Rüggle	..	1	22	26	18
,,	Torino	Rev. Benjamin Pons	1	..	108	230	190
,,	Pinerolo	Rev. Philip Cardon	1	..	110	49	35
LIGURIA	Genoa	Rev. Mattheo Prochet	1	..	150	50	75
,,	San Pier d'Arena	Rev. A. B. Tron	1	..	22	25	10
,,	Favale	Sig. Stefano Cereghino	..	1	27	19	13

Region	Station	Minister					
LOMBARDY	Milan	Rev. Jn. David Turin	1	..	125	20	65
,,	Como and	} Rev. Daniel Gay	1	..	42	17	13
,,	Val d'Intelvi		..	..	28	..	..
,,	Brescia and	} Rev. John Pons(1) }	1	..	42	..	17
,,	Castiglione delle Stiviere		..	..	16	..	6
,,	Guidizzolo	Sig. P. Forneron	..	1	13	18	24
VENETIA	Venice	Rev. John B. Pons(2)	1	..	225	103	96
,,	Verona	Rev. John Pons	1	..	40	12	18
EMILIA	Guastalla	Rev. B. Gardiol	1	..	51	28	26
THE MARCHES	Ancona	Sigs. Calvino & Vittorini	..	2	30	..	..
COMARCA	Rome	{ Rev. John Ribetti	1	..	68	76	45
		Rev. Henry Meille	1	..			
NEAPOLITAN TERRITORY	Naples	{ Rev. M. Devita	1	..	150	129	40
		Sig. Henry Tron	..	1			
,,	Fragneto		..	..	8	..	..
,,	San Bartolommeo	Sig. Falletti	..	1	14	..	..
SICILY	Catania	{ Rev. Emilio Long }	1	1	50	30	40
		Sig. A. Bellecci					
,,	Messina	{ Rev. Augustus Malan }	1	1	93	20	34
		Sig. G. G. Trom					
,,	Palermo	{ Rev. John S. Kay }	1	1	67	78	36
		Sig. E. Bosio					
,,	Trabia	Sig. S. Trapani	..	1	7	44	24
,,	Trapani	Sig. G. Fasulo	..	1	2	..	15
,,	Riesi	Rev. E. Long, temporarily	1	..	..	..	..
TUSCANY	Florence	{ Rev. Auguste Meille, Rev. Professors Geymonat, A. Revel, and E. Comba }	4	..	52	120	38
,,	Pisa	Rev. P. Weitzecker	1	..	60	26	20
,,	Lucca	Supplied from Florence temporarily	..	..	38	22	8
,,	Leghorn	Rev. P. Rostagno	1	..	78	236	130
,,	Rio Marina, Elba	Rev. S. Bonnetto	1	..	70	158	22
	40 Stations.		24	16	1952	1568	1086

From this it will be seen that the Waldensian Church has at this moment forty stations and forty missionaries labouring in Italy and Sicily, of whom twenty-four are ordained ministers who have attended the college curriculum of nine years required by the Waldensian Church, four are probationers who have also attended their whole college course, and only wait till their year of probation as missionaries has expired to be also ordained, and the other twelve are lay evangelists, or schoolmaster evangelists, who have given satisfactory proof of their piety and ability to teach. The number of day schools instituted in connection with these mission stations is fifty-eight, taught by fifty-nine teachers, and attended by 1,568 pupils, according to the return made to the Synod in August, though I am inclined to think that there has been an increase in the number since then. There are thirty-eight Sabbath schools, at which there has been an attendance of 1,086 scholars, the greater number of whom are children of parents still professing Catholicism. The congregations begin to recognise the obligation of doing something to support divine ordinances among themselves, and this year they have contributed to the funds of the Evangelization Commission the sum of 21,217,84 lires, about £848 sterling, being upwards of £400 sterling more than last year. The number of communicants up to the middle of August was 1,952, and that of catechumens 214, while the number of hearers was then stated at Sabbath worship at a maximum of 3,220. This is a brief account of the mission-work of the Waldensian Church in Italy, apart altogether from the pastoral and educational work carried on in the fifteen parishes of the valleys, and in the college of La Tour, which I have not time to enlarge on at present.

But whilst I desire to evoke the sympathy of English-speaking Christians everywhere on behalf of the Italian mission-work of the Waldensian Church, my chief object in sending out this little volume has been to call attention to some wants of the Vaudois in their own home-field. It is delightful to an English visitor to those valleys to recount the long lines of deserved connection between his own country and this Goshen of the Alps—a line reaching from the days of our first Charles, strengthening visibly during the time of Cromwell, revived under William and Mary, and Ann, continuing still through the time of the Georges; though suspended for awhile by the interference of European warfare, yet again rekindled by the energy and eloquence of Gilly, expanded and deepened by the devotedness of Beckwith, and other benefactors following in his train too numerous for us to register, but not one of them ignored or forgotten by the grateful valley-men benefitted by their Christian kindness. Apart from the institutions to which I have already adverted, there is another which meets the eye of the visitor at La Torre, as he turns up the Val Angrogna. This is the Vaudois Orphan Asylum and Industrial School, established by the British Ladies' Association, the secretary of which is Miss Hathaway, Cheltenham. As the title indicates, the orphans are taught useful industries, such as straw-hat plaiting, lace and needle-work. Articles thus made are disposed of for the benefit of the institution, which provides a home for sixty children. Very great was the need of such a place in the valleys, and deeply encouraging have been the fruits of this work of faith and labour of love. Not to extend my little book too far beyond its original design, viz., that of a "handy-book on the valleys brought down to date," I can only add that it seems to me that the chief wants of the church in her own valleys are—first, a better sustenance for her pastors; the very circumstance that those pastors are now expected to take their places side by side with the foremost men of other churches in the Continent of Europe for the defence and spread of God's truth justifies this plea, if it were otherwise weak, which it is not.

Secondly, help in the restoration of her ancient sanctuaries, and one or two additional ones. One thing that struck me as a painful void was, the absence of any public monument of the past events of the wonderful history of the Vaudois. It is true, in one sense, that the whole place is a museum of relics; that every rock has some thrilling tale, every mountain slope and hill-side graven upon it the memory of saints and martyrs. Yet I confess that those who do remember what has passed, and that those who wish that generations yet to come may know the history of these valleys, may well desire that some external tokens stood out to impress the passer-by with suitable emotion. I had this feeling most strongly as I reached the Shiloh of the valleys—the Pra del Tor.

Our route lay through the luxuriant and lovely Val Angrogna, which now rejoiced in the fascinating charms of springtide. Everywhere the eye rested on scenes of softness and beauty, the turf not unlike that which gives such a charm to an English landscape, while the undulating slopes were covered with an unutterable profusion of flowers. As we advanced higher up the valley we were strongly reminded of the words of a French writer: "Sometimes in leaving a gorge our attention was absorbed by a beautiful meadow. A strange intermixture of wild and cultivated nature met our eye everywhere, betraying the hand of man where one would have thought it impossible for him to penetrate. By the side of a cavern we find houses; branches of the vine where we only looked for brambles; vineyards in desert places, and fields amidst the overhanging rocks." All this is true beyond exaggeration, especially after you leave the village of Angrogna, with its parsonage-house in the most picturesque situation of any we encountered. About half an hour from this spot the scenery becomes wildly grand, especially as you draw nigh to the torrent. On one side is the lofty Vandalin, and on the other precipitous rocks; while in the narrow valley the stream rushes down with its roar and foam, forming beautiful cascades, and reminding you of some of the grandest scenery in Switzerland. But, greatly as I was delighted with the topographical interest of my journey, yet I would not forget that it was the people and their fathers' deeds and sufferings that had led me to undertake this rather fatiguing enterprise; and long before I reached the Barricata, or Pra del Torno, I had a great enjoyment in being taken by a Vaudois mechanic, who left his work at Angrogna, and would have no acknowledgment but my thanks, in order to show me one of those wonderful hiding-places in the very heart of the mountains, where the God of the hill and of the Vaudois so effectively succoured his people. The particular cavern I was shown was most difficult of access, not only by its seclusion, but also on other grounds; the entrance would only admit one or two persons at a time; but once within there seemed space enough for about a hundred persons. Here I understood large numbers of the persecuted Vaudois had found a refuge and a sanctuary in its holiest and happiest sense. The words, "He shall dwell on high: his place of defence shall be the munitions of rocks," came to my thoughts with a freshness and fulness of meaning not previously realized. But the testimony of this valley is everywhere, "The Lord fought for Israel." The next point of remarkable interest shows this, viz., the Barricata, which is a kind of entrance to the enclosure known as Pra del Torno. At this spot the rocks on either side come down close to the mountain, so that only a mere ledge of rock remains as a path. Consequently, a small number of men could at this point drive back a host; and here, during the persecutions of the fifteenth, sixteenth, and seventeenth centuries, the contemptuous foes of the Vaudois met with humiliating and disastrous repulses, while the Vaudois themselves escaped comparatively unhurt. This circumstance led the enemy, during the persecution of 1560, under the Count de la Trinita, to place his men on the heights above Roccamanente; but his one thousand two hundred men were successfully driven back by less than one-twentieth of that number of the Vaudois; and when he renewed the attack with scornful assurance of victory, a few days later, the Vaudois, who were engaged in prayer at the time, having despatched six of their number, who were slingers, to a commanding point above the assailants, obtained a still more triumphant victory, without loss on their own side, but with terrible slaughter to the enemy, including eight of his chief officers.

Time fails to recount all that might be said of these celebrated regions. I must, however, make passing mention of the beautiful mountain peak a little higher up on the right hand as you approach Pra del Torno, *i.e.*, La Vachera. On the 11th of June, 1655, after the Piedmontese troops were unable to force the Barricata, though they tried from 5 a.m. to 3 p.m., they advanced towards La Vachera. The Vaudois went up higher. Thinking this to be a retreat, the Piedmontese soldiers exclaimed, "Advance, wreck of Janavello!" The Vaudois responded, "Advance, wreck of San Segonzo!" accompanied by such a shower of stones that the soldiers fled in greatest confusion, leaving behind them two hundred dead, and carrying away more than twice that number of wounded. Indeed, this defeat was so decisive that the persecutors were constrained to acknowledge "God was with the Barbets," and that whereas "formerly the wolves eat the dogs (*i.e.*, barbetti), now the dogs (barbetti) eat the wolves."

But we now come to the goal of our journey to-day, Pra del Torno, a very sanctuary, embosomed amidst the everlasting hills, the site of the ancient college of the Vaudois clergy, from whence they went forth to preach the doctrines of a pure faith even before Wickliffe rose as the morning star of the Reformation in our own land. Nature is still there in all its grandeur; but I must confess to a feeling of sadness as I beheld a church under the patronage of the Virgin Mary in these valleys, where so much noble blood had been shed for the maintenance of the truth as it is in Jesus, but no place of worship for the descendants of the men who were ready to die, but not ready to dishonour God by participating in a worship contrary to His blessed Word. And my regret was not lessened when I learnt that the evangelical Vaudois has to make an eight hours' journey to his nearest temple, and that his pastor would have a journey of similar character to make to the sick and aged members of his flock in this secluded spot. I found a schoolroom, erected by General Beckwith, in a dilapidated state, and the poor old schoolmaster very infirm from sickness and age. My desire, therefore, is to raise funds either to greatly improve the schoolroom, or, better still, to erect a neat temple in this consecrated spot, so as at once to commemorate the piety and heroism of the dead, and to provide for the wants of the living. The pastor of the parish, the Rev. J. Durand Canton, has informed me how great a boon such a place would be. The Table have also assured me of their hearty co-operation. Several subscriptions have been kindly promised. F. A. Bevan, Esq., of the firm of Messrs. Barclay, Bevan, and Co., 54, Lombard Street, has kindly consented to receive donations for the object: they may also be sent to me. Let each reader of this volume join in the work, and so, by the divine blessing, it shall be accomplished; and another object also, viz., that which makes the church of the valleys a holy bond of union between Christian brethren in both hemispheres; and between those whose church polity may differ, but whose creed is one in all essential points, and who proclaim as the one thing needful a living faith in a living Saviour, the one Mediator between God and men, the man CHRIST JESUS.

Milton Keynes UK
Ingram Content Group UK Ltd.
UKHW030838021124
450589UK00006B/683

9 789362 925121